R
& Upper
Normandy

Andrew Sanger

Credits

Footprint credits
Editor: Ria Gane
Production and layout: Emma Bryers
Maps: Kevin Feeney
Cover: Pepi Bluck

Publisher: Patrick Dawson
Managing Editor: Felicity Laughton
Advertising: Elizabeth Taylor
Sales and marketing: Kirsty Holmes

Photography credits
Front cover: Anneka/Shutterstock.com
Back cover: Topora/Shutterstock.com

Printed in Great Britain by CPI Antony Rowe,
Chippenham, Wiltshire

Every effort has been made to ensure that
the facts in this guidebook are accurate.
However, travellers should still obtain advice
from consulates, airlines, etc, about travel
and visa requirements before travelling.
The authors and publishers cannot accept
responsibility for any loss, injury or
inconvenience however caused.

Publishing information
Footprint *Focus Rouen & Upper Normandy*
1st edition
© Footprint Handbooks Ltd
February 2013

ISBN: 978 1 909268 12 8
CIP DATA: A catalogue record for this book
is available from the British Library

® Footprint Handbooks and the Footprint
mark are a registered trademark of
Footprint Handbooks Ltd

Published by Footprint
6 Riverside Court
Lower Bristol Road
Bath BA2 3DZ, UK
T +44 (0)1225 469141
F +44 (0)1225 469461
footprinttravelguides.com

Distributed in the USA by Globe Pequot
Press, Guilford, Connecticut

The content of Footprint *Focus Rouen &
Upper Normandy* has been taken directly
from Footprint's *Normandy* guide which was
researched and written by Andrew Sanger.

Contents

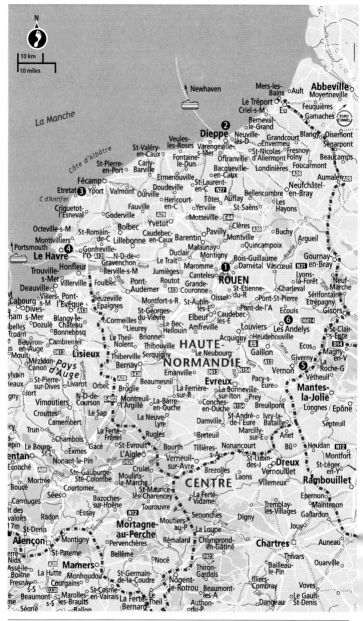

4 • Rouen & Upper Normandy

Although it has the thriving city of Rouen at its centre, Upper Normandy – like the rest of the duchy – is for the most part tranquil, picturesque and profoundly rural. It has long been a place of high art and culture, too, especially along the shores of the River Seine.

Upper Normandy is made up of the *départements* of Seine-Maritime, which climbs from the right bank of the River Seine, and Eure, most of which lies on the left bank. Between the two *départements*, the wide river makes its way to the sea in great meandering twists and turns, along which the Vikings once rowed deep into the territory of the Franks.

It was the Vikings who brought Normandy into being, having been given this territory as a duchy, and it was here that they began to develop a distinctive Norman style of design and architecture. Some of Normandy's greatest Romanesque and Gothic buildings stand on its banks or close by.

The Seine also played a key role in the birth of modern art, as the Impressionists gathered here to capture on canvas the pearly skies over the river and its estuary. Many towns of Upper Normandy, especially the coastal resorts, make a frequent appearance in early Impressionist works now hanging in museums and galleries around the world. Claude Monet, the 'Father of Impressionism', grew up in Le Havre, and lived his last years, beside the river which had inspired him, at Giverny.

Away from the river and sea coast, and its waterside towns and cities, Upper Normandy is mainly high plateau country with a patchwork of fields under wide skies, where life is quietly rustic and resolutely traditional.

Planning your trip

Places to visit in Rouen and Upper Normandy

The Seine Valley
The meandering Seine flows between forests and cliffs, abbeys and hilltop castles. On its the banks, or not far from them, stand the cities of Rouen and Le Havre, and other long-established towns, ancient abbeys, medieval castles, forests and some of the greatest landmarks of Normandy's cultural heritage, like Monet's house and garden at Giverny.

The Coast
Upper Normandy meets the English Channel in spectacular white cliffs, busy harbours and the charming pre-War resorts of the Alabaster Coast, such as Etretat and Fécamp, as well as bustling centres like the popular port and market-town of Dieppe. And on the shores of the Seine Bay, extending west of Le Havre to Caen, are chic beach resorts and bustling ports that have attracted visitors for over a century.

Rouen
Once capital of the whole Duchy, now capital of the Haute Normandie (Upper Normandy) region, historic Rouen is one of the most attractive places in Northern France. In the old heart of the city, on the river Seine's north bank, cobbled lanes ramble among exquisite houses of timber, stone, and a dozen lace-delicate Gothic churches. From the exuberant Flamboyant cathedral – which was painted again and again by Claude Monet – the old quarter's narrow main street, rue du Gros Horloge, straddled by a gilded medieval clock tower, runs into place du Vieux Marché, where Joan of Arc was burnt alive in 1431. The city makes much of its connection to St Joan and has a remarkable modern church dedicated to her.

With an array of good museums, public gardens and remnants of its long history, there's a tremendous amount to do and see in the city, from the Fine Arts Museum where a string of rooms is devoted to the Impressionists who loved this area so much and a world-class collection of Flemish art is sited, to Rouen's other great pleasures – strolling, shopping and sampling Normandy's gourmet treats.

Getting to Rouen and Upper Normandy

Air
From the UK and Ireland   The only international direct flight to Normandy is the one hour journey from London City airport to Deauville, operated by **CityJet** (cityjet.com). There are one to four departures weekly, with fares from £139 return.

The principal air gateway to the region is Paris. There are several flights daily from London Heathrow, London Luton, Edinburgh, most UK regional airports and Dublin, to France's main international airport Charles de Gaulle (CDG), 22 km north of Paris. Less frequent flights depart from London Gatwick and several other UK and Irish local airports, including Cork. A small number of flights land at Paris Orly, 15 km south of the capital, most from London City airport. Airlines operating these routes include **Aeromexico**, **Air Europa**, **Air France**, **Air Mauritius**, **Alitalia**, **American Airlines**, **British Airways**, **Delta Airlines**,

Don't miss...

EasyJet, Flybe, and **Qantas**. From Scotland or Ireland **Ryanair** fly to 'Paris' (Beauvais airport, 88 km from Rouen on N31) from Glasgow, Shannon and Dublin.

From North America Several flights depart daily from Chicago, Cincinnati, Detroit, Houston, Los Angeles, Miami, Montreal, New York, Philadelphia, San Francisco, Toronto and Washington DC to Paris Charles de Gaulle, with a less frequent service from Pittsburgh, Salt Lake City, Seattle and Vancouver.

From rest of Europe All European capitals have direct flights to Paris, and there are frequent daily flights to Paris from dozens of other European cities. Within France, internal flights connect French regional airports to the small airports at Le Havre and Rouen.

Onward travel from Paris CDG and Orly airports Seven major international car hire companies have desks at the two Paris airports. From Charles de Gaulle to Rouen is 140 km via D104, N104 and D14. Alternatively, travel by RER train into central Paris and onward from Paris-St Lazare to Rouen and other parts of Upper Normandy.

Rail

Journey time from London St Pancras to Paris Gare du Nord on **Eurostar** ① *T08705-186186, eurostar.com*, is 2¼ hours, plus a 30-minute check-in (from £69 return). Eurostar can add onward rail travel to Rouen. Change in Paris to Paris-St Lazare station (allow 1½ hours to change stations) to continue by TGV or intercity rail services to Rouen (journey time from Paris, from one hour 12 minutes, from London four hours 29 minutes, total return fare from London from £89). Time it right and you can bypass Paris by getting off Eurostar at Lille Europe station, walking 10 minutes to Lille Flandres station, and taking a train direct from there to Rouen (usually twice daily, two hours 36 minutes).

Rail travel to other destinations in Upper Normandy can be pre-booked with **Rail Europe** ① *T08448-484064, raileurope.co.uk*, in the UK or USA, or the French railway company **SNCF** ① *T08 92 35 35 35, voyages-sncf.com*, from outside France, or within France at any French train station. Catch a train at Paris-St Lazare for Dieppe, Evreux, Fécamp, Le Havre, or Rouen.

Road

Bus/coach Eurolines ① *T0871-7818181 premium rate, eurolines.co.uk*, run a service from London to Paris, from where you can take a train to Upper Normandy. The journey time is eight to nine hours and while the standard fare is £52, on certain days and times it costs as little as £17 return (including booking fees). Most buses arrive at the station of **Eurolines**

France ① *28 av Général-de-Gaulle, Bagnolet, T08 92 89 90 91, eurolines.fr*, close to the Métro station Gallieni, with a 35-minute onward journey into Paris.

Car The fastest way to travel to Upper Normandy from southeast England is by road and Eurotunnel. **Eurotunnel** ① *T08443-353 535, eurotunnel.com*, trains run from the M20 near Folkestone direct to autoroute A16 near Calais. It operates 24 hours a day with up to four departures an hour in peak times. Check-in and departure are rapid, and the crossing takes 35 minutes plus 30 minutes check-in, with little delay in unloading vehicles. Standard fares start from £64 single, £128 return, for a car and up to nine passengers. There are often promotions with lower fares on certain dates, and reductions for frequent travellers, while a five-day return costs £94. The onward driving time into Upper Normandy via autoroutes A16, A28, A29 or A13 is about two hours to Rouen (215 km).

Sea
Typical mid-week cross-Channel fares direct to Upper Normandy are given below, but look out for frequent bargain special offers. There are also crossings to the Lower Normandy ports of Caen and Cherbourg-Octeville. Cheaper, quicker and more frequent are crossings to Calais, Boulogne and Dunkerque.

To Dieppe From Newhaven **LD Lines** ① *T0800 917 1201, ldlines.co.uk*. Twice daily, crossing time four hours, plus minimum 45-minute check-in, return fare typically £141 for driver and car plus £15 per passenger.

To Le Havre From Portsmouth **LD Lines**. One crossing daily. Crossing time 5½ hours by day, eight hours at night, plus 45-minute check-in, typical return fare £173 for driver and car, plus around £15 per passenger.

Transport in Rouen and Upper Normandy

Rail
French trains are run by the state-owned **SNCF** ① *T0825-000 276, sncf.com*. As in every other French region, Upper Normandy's principal towns are connected by fast modern trains several times daily. Rail routes link towns in the north of the region, and a rail service also loops through the area south of the Seine.

   For Upper Normandy rail information, check SNCF's dedicated website for the regions, ter-sncf.com. Remember that on the website, Upper Normandy is called by its French name, Haute Normandie, which has its own pages at ter-sncf.com/haute_normandie. There's a map of the complete SNCF network in Upper Normandy at ter-sncf.com/haute_normandie/carte_horaires/index.asp.

Rouen The main rail route into Upper Normandy is Paris to Rouen (from one hour 11 minutes). Rouen also has main line rail connections to Caen and Cherbourg-Octeville in Lower Normandy.

Dieppe and Le Havre There are rail services from Rouen to Le Havre (51 minutes) and Dieppe (45 minutes).

Côte d'Albâtre There is a service between Le Havre and Fécamp (40 minutes).

Road

Bicycle Picturesque countryside, quiet country lanes and gently challenging topography make Upper Normandy a good region for cycling. Long-distance cycle routes cut through the region, including the Voies Vertes (green ways), former railway lines. Local trains within Upper Normandy transport bikes free of charge, without pre-booking, in the luggage compartment.

IGN Cartes de Promenade maps, intended for walkers, are useful. IGN Serie Bleue maps cover a smaller area in more detail. Most tourist offices have information about cycle trails in their area, and can give the addresses of local bike hire firms – usually at least one in every town. Many focus on VTT (mountain bikes) but it is also possible to hire touring cycles. Shop around, as hire fees vary considerably. Expect to pay around €100 a week or €20 a day for a touring bike, or €120 a week, €25 day, for a mountain bike. Prices for children's bikes are likely to be almost as much.

The city of Rouen operates a free bike scheme, called Cy'clic. This gives 30 minutes' free hire, followed by increasing charges for subsequent periods. You have to register for the scheme, and use your credit card to pick up the sturdy roadsters from stands all around town.

Bus/coach Local bus network tend to have timetables geared to the needs of workers and schoolchildren. Most do not cross the départemental boundary. Out-of-town sights can be hard to reach by public bus. National rail operator **SNCF** ① *T0825 000 276, ter-sncf. com/haute_normandie*, also runs bus routes to supplement train services; these are shown on railway timetables. An SNCF bus, for example, links Rouen directly to Evreux (one hour). There is a flat fare of just €2 for all bus journeys throughout Upper Normandy.

There is little public transport between towns along the Côte d'Albâtre between Fécamp, Dieppe and Le Tréport. Regular bus services between Etretat, Fécamp and Le Havre are operated by **Cars Périer** ① *T02 35 46 37 77, cars-perier.com*.

Car Travelling by car makes it easy and enjoyable to explore Normandy's rural areas. However, with autoroute tolls and fuel costing about €1.50 per litre, driving has become a more expensive option. In addition, traffic congestion, traffic-free streets, and finding somewhere to park all make car travel difficult in main towns, especially Rouen.

Speed limits are generally 110 kph (68 mph) on dual carriageways, and 130 kph (80 mph) on motorways (sometimes lower on toll-free motorways). Otherwise, the maximum speed is generally 50 kph (31 mph) in town, 90 kph (55 mph) out of town. Insurance documents, car registration papers and a full driving licence issued by any EU country or the US must be carried when driving. Third party insurance is compulsory. Comprehensive insurance issued by UK insurers is valid throughout the EU (a so-called Green Card is no longer required). The minimum driving age for a car or motorcycle is 18.

By law you must stop immediately after an accident, with minimum obstruction to traffic. If anyone has been injured, or is under the influence of alcohol, call the police. French motorists must complete an insurance form verifying the facts and all parties must sign to show that they agree that it is a true account. Non-French motorists should exchange details with the other parties. If you break down, put on hazard warning lights (or display a warning triangle). Misunderstanding this important rule is the main cause of accidents involving foreign motorists in France. Drive on the right and *always give way to anything approaching from the right*, except where signs indicate to the contrary. The main priority signs are a rectangular yellow sign if you have priority, and a yellow rectangle crossed out meaning you no longer have priority. Where two major roads merge, look out for signs showing who has priority (*Vous n'avez pas la priorité* and/or *Cédez le passage*). Two important exceptions are that vehicles emerging from private property don't have priority over traffic on the public highway, and most roundabouts give priority to vehicles already in the roundabout (as in the UK).

Police levy hefty on-the-spot fines for speeding, worn tyres, not wearing a seat belt, not stopping at a Stop sign and overtaking where forbidden. The amount is likely to be about €135, but can be considerably more depending on the circumstances. Issuing a receipt is part of the on-the-spot procedure – always be sure to get one, and keep it carefully. Serious violations such as drink-driving could lead to your car being impounded, as well as heavy fines or imprisonment.

Service stations, especially on autoroutes, sell a range of excellent road atlases and maps, including the well-respected Michelin and IGN. **Bison Futé** ① *bison-fute. equipement.gouv.fr*, publish an annual map showing less congested itineraries, free from tourist offices and gas stations.

Parking meter charges are relatively modest, but it can be difficult finding a space. Payment is required typically Monday-Friday 0900-1800, Saturday 0900-1200. A good time to find a parking space is lunchtime (1200-1400) and there's often no charge for parking then. Parking spaces painted with blue lines are Zone Bleue, where parking is free for 90 minutes if the time of arrival is displayed in the windscreen with a '*disque horaire pour les zones bleue*', known as a Disque Bleue. Blue EU Disabled Parking photocards issued in the UK are valid in France, but in a Zone Bleue must be used in conjunction with a Disque Bleue.

Car hire is widely available from both international and local firms. At airports, stations and main roads in the cities and resorts you'll see all the familiar car rental names. Prices are generally higher than in other countries, especially for drivers under 25. Before signing the rental agreement, check that any existing damage on a vehicle you are about to rent has been noted. Make sure your rental is for unlimited mileage – some firms may place an upper limit on the free mileage. Be sure to return the car with the same amount of fuel as at the start of the rental, as fuel charges may be imposed by car rental companies.

Where to stay in Rouen and Upper Normandy

Chic pre-war resorts, family beach holidays, lively city breaks and simple country living are all among the favourite holiday options here. Upper Normandy appeals to a very wide range of people and interests, with a diverse choice of accommodation to match.

Prices

Many visitors to Upper Normandy are travelling on a package holiday – that is, accommodation and transport (and sometimes meals) combined in an inclusive price, pre-booked with a travel agent or tour operator in their home country. This is normally cheaper and easier than paying for each element of the trip separately. However, package deals usually require a minimum stay of three nights in a hotel, or a week in self-catering or campsite accommodation. You may also be required to arrive at your accommodation on a particular 'changeover day'.

For more freedom and independence, especially on a touring holiday with a flexible itinerary, you may need to find and book accommodation yourself. This is not difficult: the internet has made it easy to make reservations in advance.

Price codes

Where to stay

€€€€ over €200   €€€ €101-200

€€ €60-100   € under €60

Price codes refer to the cost of a double room in high season.

Restaurants

€€€ over €40   €€ €20-40   € under €20

Price codes refer to the cost of a two-course meal with a drink for one person, including service and cover charge.

Hotel pricing in France is normally for the room, not per person. Breakfast is generally not included, but is available for an extra charge of about €12-15 in mid-priced establishments – it is usually cheaper to pop out to a café.

Hotels are graded with a star system, but some hotels fall short of a single star (expect to pay under €40), while others far exceed the requirements. For France's maximum grade 'four-star Luxe' expect to pay over €300 per night. Most have three stars (around €90-150 per double room).

Prices vary considerably by season and from place to place. Prices take a big step up as the summer peak approaches. Expect to see room rates rise sharply at Easter, then in June, and again in July. They step down again at the end of August, making early autumn a good time to visit.

Booking

To visit the most popular parts of Normandy during peak season (July-August), it's wise to plan everything at least two months in advance. Out of high season, though, especially away from the main towns, it is not usually necessary to book more than a day in advance.

Hotels and *chambres d'hôtes* (guest rooms) are easily booked online or by phone. For small, independent, family-run establishments, especially off the beaten track, a smattering of French may be needed. For camping and self-catering, it can be simpler to pre-book a package rather than to arrange independently.

Hotels

In and around Normandy's larger towns, you will find everything from predictable, decent budget hotels to stylish four-star Luxe hotels. Almost all towns and many villages have at least one modest, comfortable three-star hotel, generally with its own restaurant. They often have a traditional feel and are sometimes in historic mansions and manor houses (do ask in advance if steep stairs or other access issues may be a problem). If prices are very low, ask carefully about facilities – a bargain-priced hotel room may lack modern amenities.

The major international hotel groups are all present. In addition, the big French chains, all with several hotels in the region, include **Campanile** motels with restaurants, economy motels such as **Formule 1**, which are modern and simple, **Ibis** (functional, budget-priced town hotels), and more upmarket chains **Meridien** and **Sofitel**.

A high proportion of hotels are independent, most of which belong to hotel federations that resemble chains, requiring member establishments to reach a certain standard. Two dependable French hotel and restaurant federations are **Relais &**

Châteaux, which offer classic luxury, and **Logis de France**, small, traditional family-run hotels, nearly all with a restaurant.

B&B/chambres d'hôtes
Bed and breakfast accommodation in private homes (usually in a purpose-built extension) is common in rural areas. It provides an inexpensive alternative with the added interest of meeting local people and getting under the surface of Normandy life. These *chambres d'hôtes* (guest rooms) often have a simple sign on the front gate. You're welcome to stop and ask for a room. They often provide an evening meal too. All cd'hôtes have to be approved by local authorities.

Gîtes/self-catering
Gîtes – self-catering country cottages – are found all over Upper Normandy in the most rural areas. They're often a bargain, though facilities can be old-fashioned. It is wise to pre-book, either by phone or online (gites-de-france.fr, in French and English).

For self-catering with all the comforts of home, choose from thousands of modern holiday houses and villas available from a number of UK tour operators and agencies. You can find self-catering in towns, too: *meublés* ('furnished') are vacation apartments. Contact local tourist offices for a list; they can also make bookings.

Campsites
Campsites are the least expensive accommodation and often in the best locations. Most of the larger sites have a number of erected spacious modern tents as well as rows of mobile homes fixed in position. Campsites are carefully regulated and must meet approved standards. They're graded with stars: anything with two or more stars has hot showers and good facilities. Four-star and the even better four-star 'Grand Comfort' sites have excellent amenities, often including a swimming pool. *Camping à la Ferme*, campsites on farms, are a category on their own that tends to be more basic. At the other extreme, **Castels et Camping**, mainly in superb locations, is a federation of top-quality camps.

Food and drink in Rouen and Upper Normandy

Gastronomic region
French tourists happily make their way to Normandy for the pleasures of the table. Normandy's traditional cooking has a highly distinctive regional style, with a strong emphasis on its rich dairy produce, shellfish and good-quality meats, as well as the abundant harvest of its cherry, pear and especially apple orchards.

There are numerous Normandy specialities. The result of all those orchards and dairy farms and picturesque fishing harbours is meals with plenty of local cheeses, butter, and thick, farm-made, semi-sour crème fraîche for savoury cream sauces. Apples may turn up in any course as apple sauces and apple pastry, dry cider and fiery Calvados, and the sherry-like aperitif, *pommeau*.

More than that, Normandy is renowned in France for the sheer size of meals. Normans are trenchermen *par excellence*, spending longer at the table than anyone else in the country. From this arose the tradition of the *trou normand* – literally the 'Norman gap', but the custom itself is more elegant than the phrase: a short break between two main courses, in which a tot of Calvados is sipped, supposedly to aid digestion. Nowadays it is more likely to be a Calvados sorbet.

Dining tips

Choose a prix-fixe menu
At most restaurants you'll be offered à la carte (list of dishes, individually priced) and a choice of about three menus, that is, *prix fixe* (fixed price) set meals. Typical menu prices might be €20-40. The price difference reflects not differences in quality but in number of courses and difficulty of preparation. In general, to get the best out of a restaurant, and the best value for money, order one of the menus, not à la carte.

Formula for a cheap lunch
For a quick light meal, many restaurants and bars offer an inexpensive fixed-price *formule* without specifying the dishes. It's often a starter and simple main course, or main course and dessert, with a quarter-litre of house wine and a coffee.

What's on the bill?
French restaurant prices always include service and all taxes. It's not necessary to give any extra tip. *Vin compris* means wine included (usually a quarter of a litre of house wine per person); *boisson comprise* means you may have a beer or soft drink instead.

Eat at the right time
Away from resorts and big cities, it can be difficult to find something to eat outside normal mealtimes. Lunch is generally served 1200-1400 (Sunday lunch lasts until 1500), and dinner 1900-2200.

Out of hours dining
Brasseries (breweries) are bars that serve food at any time of day. A *salon de thé* is a smarter alternative for between-meals pastries and other light snacks with tea or coffee.

No need to dress for dinner
Smart casual is the norm in even the best places, though you may dress up if you prefer.

Dairy produce
Some of the best-known French cheeses come from Normandy. Creamy and pungent 'washed-rind' boxed cheeses, made from the milk of grass-fed cows, carry the names of the towns and villages where they were first produced. Among them are Camembert, Pont l'Évêque, Livarot and Pavé d'Auge, all in the Pays d'Auge just south of the Seine, and from the north side, Neufchâtel (which is usually made in a cute heart shape). Local farm-made crème fraîche is a staple of Normandy's all-important sauces: a rich, smooth, slightly soured thick cream. Normandy butter, processed and wrapped at Isigny, is also counted among the very best and is widely exported all over France and abroad.

Seafood
Expect to find lobsters and crayfish, crabs and spider crabs, oysters, scallops and mussels on almost every menu. They are jointly known as *fruits de mer* and often served in large heaps. Such seafood is another essential ingredient of Normandy's sauces and stews.

Local specialities

Almost every good meal in Normandy includes lashings of cream and a good splash of Calvados or cider. Among the most famous of all Normandy's plethora of local specialities is *tripes à la mode de Caen*, a long-cooked stew of tripe, pig's trotters, vegetables, herbs and Calvados. Another is *Marmite Dieppoise*, a creamy fish-and-shellfish stew supposedly invented at the restaurant from which it takes its name. More generally, *dieppoise*, as in the classic *sole à la dieppoise*, means served in a creamy sauce made with white wine, mussels and crayfish. Other local favourites include charcuterie, especially *andouilles* and *andouillettes* (chitterling sausages large and small) from the farms of south-western Calvados, and *boudin* (black pudding) from Le Perche. *Agneau de pré-salé* is the distinctive-tasting tender lamb from the flood meadows around Mont St Michel Bay.

For something simple, crèpes have long been Normandy's preferred cheap snack. These paper-thin pancakes can be sprinkled with almost anything, sweet or savoury. To finish the meal, apples, pears and cherries are served in tasty flans and tarts.

Festivals in Rouen and Upper Normandy

Normandy's calendar reflects the two great preoccupations of the duchy and its people – good food and the sea. From spring to autumn, food fairs celebrate local produce, and traditional blessings are made for the sea and those who work on it. There are also prestigious arts and music festivals.

May and June
Bénédiction de la Mer (**May, on Ascension Day**) A devout traditional procession in Etretat to a seashore Mass and a cliff-top blessing.
Fête de Ste Jeanne d'Arc (**Sun nearest 30 May**) This festival in Rouen is both solemn and festive, with religious services but also medieval markets and street theatre (rouentourisme.com).
Pentecôte (**May or Jun**) The religious holiday of Pentecost (or Whitsun) is a holiday weekend in France.

September
Fête du Cidre (**end of Sep**) A celebration of local traditions and of the local brew in Caudebec-en-Caux.

November
Foire aux Harengsor Fête du Hareng (**mid-Nov**) Herrings are celebrated at this quayside festival in Dieppe, and at most other towns on the Alabaster Coast (seine-maritime-tourisme.com).

Shopping in Rouen and Upper Normandy

Most shopping areas have excellent *perfumiers*. Other shops sell an extensive choice of attractive and affordable good-quality kitchenware, household goods and wine paraphernalia. Rouen and Le Havre have pedestrianized shopping areas packed with good shops. Some department store chains are renowned for glamour and style, especially Galeries Lafayettes, which has a branch in Rouen.

Arts and crafts
Traditional crafts and trades survive in several parts of Normandy. Knitted goods (*tricoterie*) are a tradition of the fishing ports, many of which now have fine knitwear boutiques. Look

out for antiques too, in street markets, *brocantes* (second-hand shops) and *antiquaires* (antiques dealers). You may find even discover good pieces of the 18th and 19th-century local blue and white patterned faïence and porcelain known as Rouen ware.

Clothes
Stylish fashion boutiques and small independent stores give character to the shopping streets of all Normandy's main towns. Even smaller towns keep up to date with latest French fashions. Look especially for beautiful shoes, jewellery, handbags and lingerie. Menswear shops no less than womenswear have originality and flair. There are delightful children's clothes too. Even babies are well dressed in France.

Farm produce
All over Upper Normandy, away from the big towns and resorts, quiet country roads pass farm gates with signs inviting you to a *dégustation* (tasting). On offer may be cider and other alcoholic apple drinks, and pear drinks too, as well as fresh fruit juices, cheeses, farmhouse pâtés and preserved meats, and honey from their own hives. Tastings are usually free, and there may even be a free tour too, showing how the produce is made. Although there is no obligation, etiquette requires that having tasted, you will buy – at least a small amount. Prices are usually a little less than in a supermarket. Generally, the goods are suitable for taking home, although strong cheeses should not be kept in the car too long!

Food and drink
In any Upper Normandy town you'll find busy specialist stores selling locally produced food and drink. The *traiteur* and *charcuterie* both have *boudins*, *andouillettes* and other prepared and preserved meats and ready-to-eat cooked dishes and salads. *Boucherie* is a butcher's shop. An *epicerie* stocks everyday foods, including *calvados* and cider, while the classier *epicerie fine* caters to gourmet tastes, and generally has a top-quality cheese counter, perhaps *crème fraîche* ladled from a tub and fresh butter cut from a large slab. *Boulangerie* is a baker's, often selling country-style breads as well as traditional baguette and *flute*. They may sell pastries too, but a better place for those is the *pâtisserie*, the pastry-cook's. *Chocolatiers* and *confiseurs* (or confiserie) make and sell confectionery, while a *glacier* (it sounds cold!) specialises in ice-cream. A *supermarché* is a small self-service shop, while an edge-of-town *hypermarché* – a large supermarket – will stock a full range of goods from around the world.

Markets
Most towns in Upper Normandy have at least one farmer's market (*marché*) per week, either in a centuries-old market square or a covered *halles*. Among the best of Upper Normandy's street markets are in Dieppe and Rouen. They include dozens of stalls selling inexpensive clothes, kitchenware, household items and other goods. Freshly gathered fruit and vegetables in season are piled high. Look out for stalls with local Normandy cheeses, creamy white heart shapes of Neufchâtel or squares of Livarot and Pont l'Evêque and circles of Camembert, as well as ready-to-eat stews and whole roasted free-range chickens off the spit for as little as €6, a multitude of dried sausages, jars of preserved meats and bottles of local cider and other drinks. Markets are usually held in the morning only, from about 0700 to 1300.

Seafood

At fishing ports, the fresh catch is laid out and sold each morning from stalls on the quayside. Sole, brill and mackerel are plentiful. Early in the day, you can see it being carted straight into the kitchens of waterfront restaurants. Queues of discerning locals form to buy the best of fish and shellfish, usually by the half-kilo, the kilo or even larger amounts, such as 5 kg of the popular Coquilles St Jacques (scallops) for about €20. Remember to keep live shellfish cold, but not on ice, and not in an airtight bag. Eat them within a day or two.

Essentials A-Z

Customs and immigration
UK and other EU citizens do not need a visa to visit France. Travellers from USA, Australia, New Zealand and Canada may stay up to 90 days without a visa. There are no restrictions on importing legal articles for personal use.

Disabled travellers
France is aware of the needs of disabled travellers but provision for them is patchy. New public buildings are obliged to provide access and facilities, but problems can be acute in areas with cobbled paving and medieval buildings. For parking, display your EU blue photocard as in the UK. French organizations for the disabled focus on residents, not tourists. Normandy Tourism produces useful booklets (in French, but using easy-to-understand symbols) detailing tourist establishments with facilities for the disabled. They are available online at normandie-tourisme. fr/normandy-tourism/more-information/ disabled-friendly-normandy-179-2.html.

Etiquette
Most French people rigorously observe conventions of politeness, always shaking hands on first introduction, moving on to kisses on the cheek (2, 3 or 4 depending on the nature of the relationship) with friends. The formal word *vous* should be used for 'you' until a fine line of intimacy has been crossed, then you should stick to *tu*. Punctuality is fairly strictly observed. Dress in public places is usually smart casual and stylish. Address strangers as *Monsieur*, *Madame* or *Mademoiselle*. Entering or leaving small shops or offices, especially in rural areas, greet those inside with a quick '*Messieurs-dames*'.

Children
Upper Normandy, like most regions of France, is extremely family friendly. Children are welcomed in restaurants with their own menu. Hotels often have family rooms, or can wheel in an extra cot or bed for a few euros extra. Discounts are usually offered at sights and attractions.

Electricity
The power is supply in France is 220 volts. Circular 2-pin plugs are used.

Health
Comprehensive travel and medical insurance is recommended. EU citizens should apply for a free **European Health Insurance Card** or EHIC (ehic.org), which entitles you to emergency medical treatment on the same terms as French nationals. Note that you will have to pay all charges and prescriptions up front and be reimbursed once you return home. If you develop a minor ailment while on holiday a visit to any pharmacy will allow you to discuss your concerns with highly qualified staff, who can give medical advice and recommend treatment. Outside normal opening hours, the address of the nearest duty pharmacy (*pharmacie de garde*) is displayed in the pharmacy window. The out-of-hours number for a local doctor (*médecin généraliste*) may also be listed.

In a serious emergency, go to the accident and emergency department (*urgences*) at the nearest Centre Hospitalier (numbers listed at the end of each chapter) or call an ambulance (SAMU) by dialling 15.

Insurance
Comprehensive travel and medical insurance is strongly recommended, as the **European Health Insurance Card** (EHIC) does not cover medical repatriation, ongoing medical treatment or treatment

considered to be non-urgent. Check for exclusions if you mean to engage in risky sports. Keep all insurance documents to hand; a good way to keep track of your policies is to email the details to yourself. Make sure you have adequate insurance when hiring a car and always ask how much excess you are liable for if the vehicle is returned with any damage. It is generally worth paying a little more for collision damage waiver. If driving your own vehicle to France, contact your insurers before you travel to ensure you are adequately covered, and keep the documents in your vehicle in case you need to prove it.

Money
The French currency is the Euro (€). Euros are available from ATMs using credit or debit cards. Credit cards are widely accepted by shops, restaurants, museums, attractions, petrol stations, etc, but may be refused in shops for purchases below about €5. Remember you need your PIN for every transaction. Cash is needed for buses, taxis, bars and markets.

Opening hours
Few shops open on Sun in France and many shops are also closed on Mon. The exception is in popular tourist centres and resorts. Most town centre shops are open Tue-Sat 0900-1200 or 1230 and 1400-1430-1800. Food shops often open earlier in the morning, and a few (especially *boulangeries* and *pâtisseries*) open on Sun morning. Most stores usually open Mon-Sat 0900-1830, but often have one or more late evening mid-week. Hypermarkets are normally open Mon-Sat 0900-2200.

Police
To call police in an emergency, dial 17. French police are divided into different forces with different roles. *Gendarmes* are armed units on call to deal with crime, especially outside urban areas. *Police Nationale* are ordinary employees under the control of the mayor, dealing with routine policing issues. CRS have a wide remit to prevent violent civil disturbance.

Post
The post office (PTT, or La Poste) provides communications services, generally including stamps, phone and internet access. Offices are open (with local variations) during normal working hours Mon-Fri, and usually Sat morning. Stamps (*timbres*) can also be bought in newsagents and little stores known as tabacs. A stamp for an ordinary letter (up to 20 g) or postcard within France costs €0.57; within the EU €0.77; to the US, Canada, Australia and most other countries €0.89. Letter boxes are yellow.

Safety
All towns and rural areas in Upper Normandy are generally safe, with little crime. However, sensible precautions should be taken; for example, don't leave anything valuable on view in cars.

Telephone
French phone numbers indicate which region and which town they are in (all Normandy numbers begin with 02, for example), but there are no area codes and you must dial all 10 digits when phoning from inside France. The prefix for France is +33 and drop the initial 0 of the number you are phoning. For international operator assistance, dial 3212.

France is well covered by mobile phone (cell phone) reception. European (including UK) visitors can use their phones normally. Visitors from the US and Australia should call their provider to check their package. On arrival in France you will receive a text informing you of the charges. All public phones required a pre-paid card, available from newsagents, tabacs, etc.

Time

France uses Central European Standard Time
and Central European Daylight Saving Time
(ie GMT+1 and GMT+2 respectively). CET
Daylight Saving Time (Summer Time) starts
at 0200 on the last Sun in Mar and ends at
0300 on the last Sun in Oct.

Tipping

Tipping is not necessary in France. Hotel,
restaurant and bar bills include service and
no tip is expected, although small change
is often left for service at an outdoor table.

Taxi drivers do not expect tips, though
many people do round the fare up.
For good service anywhere, just say '*Merci*!'

Tourist information

For regional information, contact the
Normandy Tourism (**CRT Normandie**),
T02 32 33 79 00, normandie-tourisme.fr.
For local information: Dieppe, T02 32 14
40 60, dieppetourisme.com; Giverny T02
32 51 28 22, giverny-village.fr; Le Havre
T02 32 74 04 04, lehavretourisme.com;
Rouen T02 32 08 32 40, rouentourisme.com.

Contents

Rouen

Today the modern industrial city of Rouen, sprawling on both sides of the River Seine, is the capital of the *département* of Upper Normandy. However, Rouen's standing in Normandy and in France is far greater than that.

At its very heart, on the river's right bank, is the much more ancient city from which it grew. The original capital of the Viking Duchy, previously a Roman town and still earlier a Celtic settlement, Rouen keeps intact that sense of being the first and greatest city in Normandy.

For the French nation, the name of Rouen resonates with that of Ste-Jeanne d'Arc – Joan of Arc – patron saint of France. In 1431 she was burnt alive in the city's market square, where now a church and a towering crucifix stand in memory of her life and death.

Far from being marked with tragedy by those events, Rouen is full of life and joie de vivre, its squares and streets crowded and lined with stylish shops and good restaurants.

There is superb medieval architecture. Despite extensive wartime damage, whole streets of architectural treasures survive, including hundreds of picturesque half-timbered dwellings. Soaring spires and towers rise above the rooftops. Rouen Cathedral – painted nearly 30 times by Monet (at different times of day) – is one of Europe's Gothic masterpieces.

Arriving in Rouen

Getting around

By foot Unless you have friends or business within the modern quarters of Rouen, you are unlikely to leave Vieux Rouen, the old heart of the city which contains almost everything of interest. This is a small enough area to be thoroughly explored on foot. Many city centre streets are closed to all vehicles, and several to all except public transport.

By bicycle Another transport option is the city's **Cy'clic** bike rental scheme: using your credit card, pick up a bicycle at any of 21 rental points all over town and leave it at any other rental point when you are finished. The first 30 minutes are free. See http://cyclic.rouen.fr for information.

By car Parking is a problem in Rouen. There are plenty of car parks, but they are expensive. There is free parking in place Boulingrin, and on the left bank of the Seine between Corneille and Jeanne d'Arc bridges. Public transport ticket holders may park free in the car park Parking du Mont-Riboudet.

By public transport If you do decide to go further afield, for example to the Jardin des Plantes in southern Rouen, or if you are staying on the south bank, getting around is simple. The city has an efficient, comprehensive public-transportation network. This includes metro, bus and the unusual high-tech Téor system in which wheeled buses, following visual tracks in the road, function as trams on parts of certain city centre routes. Rouen public transport is run by TCAR (**Transports en Commun de l'Agglomération de Rouen**) ① *T02-35 52 52 52 (French only), tcar.fr.* **Bus station** ① *Gare Routière, 9 rue Jeanne d'Arc.* **Train station** ① *Gare Rouen Rive Droite, at the north end of rue Jeanne d'Arc.* See page 8 for regional rail travel.

Tourist information office ① *25 place de la Cathédrale (facing the cathedral), T02-32 08 32 40, rouentourisme.com, Oct-Apr Mon-Sat 0930-1230 and 1330-1800, May-Sep Mon-Sat 0900-1900, Sun and holidays 0930-1230 and 1400-1800.* A great way to enjoy the main sights of the Old Quarter with an expert guide but at your own pace is simply to hire an audio guide. Available from Rouen tourist office, they cost just €5.

Cathedral Quarter → *For listings, see pages 32-39.*

Not for nothing is Rouen's tourist office located in place de la Cathédrale. Almost every visitor to the city makes their way to this spacious square to see with their own eyes the west front of Cathédrale Notre Dame. Despite over 800 years of eventful history, Rouen's cathedral is probably best known for one 19th-century Impressionist painter. Claude Monet sat in the square with his canvas day after day, painting the glorious Gothic stonework of the building's intricate main west façade 28 times to capture the changing moods and impressions created by changing daylight. One example can be seen in the city's Musée des Beaux Arts, but the others are scattered in the great art museums of the world. If you love Gothic architecture at its finest, linger in this quarter, for close by are two other Gothic masterpieces. The surrounding streets are full of fine domestic architecture too, with half-timbered houses dating back in some cases to the 15th century. From the cathedral, walk beside medieval dwellings along rue St-Romain to St-Maclou church, and

Rouen

N

100 metres
100 yards

R d'Herbouville
R Campulley
R Bouquet
R Maladrerie
R St-Maur
R de Blainville
R Pouchet
R St-André
R de la Martel
Rampe du Bouvreuil
Bd de la Marne
Bd de l'Yser
R du Champ des Oiseaux
R de l'Avalasse
R Bras de

Gare
Routière
Gare
SNCF
Pl Tissot
Gare Rue Verte
R Verte
R de la Rochefoucauld
R du Champ des Oiseaux

8
1
4 3
18

Musée
Antiqu
R Du

Tour
Jeanne
d'Arc
R du Donjon
R de la Glacière
R d'Ecosse
Pl du
Dr Cerné
Morand
R du Cordier
R Beauvoisine
R des Carmélites
Pl de
Rougen
R de Montbret
R de la Seille
R de la Cigogne

St-Patrice †
R St-Patrice
R Jean Lecanuet
R des Maillets
R Eloupée
R Jeanne d'Arc
R du Sacre
R du Moulinet
R du Bouvreuil
R du Bailliage
R Faucon
Musée de la
Ceramique
15
Sq
Verdrel
Musée des
Beaux Arts
Esp
Duchamp
Allée Delacroix
St-Beffroy
R du Goddard
St-Godard
Musée le
Secq des
Tournelles
R Jean Lecanuet

12
Pl
Cauchoise
R Cauchoise
R Lemery
Champs Maillets
R des Bons Enfants
R des Béguines
R de Fontenelle
R du Cercle
R de Crosne
25
4
10
R de l'Ancienne Prison
R Ste-Croix des Pelletiers
R Ecuyère
R Eau-de-Robec
16
R G le Conquérant
ATM
Palais
de Justice
14
Galerie
de l'Espace
du Palais
R Socrate
R des Fossés Louis VIII
R de l'Hôpital
R des Arsins
2
5
R des Carmes
R des Carmes
R de la Chaîne
R St-Amand

R de la Pie
Pl du
Vieux Marché
Eglise Ste-
Jeanne
d'Arc
R Rollon
22
15
17
11
9
Pl M
Foch
Palais de
Justice
R aux Juifs
R St-Lô
R St-Herbland
Croix de fer
13
R St-Nicolas
R des Chanoines

7
R du Vieux Palais
PLM
Luther King
St-Eloi
Pl
Henri IV
R St-Eloi
R André Gide
R du Général Giraud
19
Pl de
la Pucelle
d'Orléans
R du Gros Horloge
Henriette
R de la Vicomte
20
Le Gros
Horloge
R du Gros Horloge
R des Vergetiers
R Massacre
R Thouret
R du Bec
Pl de la
Cathédrale
Cathédrale
Notre-Dame
Pl St
Barthél
R de la République
R Malpalu
R St-Romain
R des Bonnetiers
11
7
Pl du
Change
5
1
R des Charrettes
Théâtre
des Arts
Opera
de Rouen
Pl des
Arts
R Dr Rambert
R Jeanne d'Arc
R C St-Saëns
R du Fardeau
R aux Ours
R du Général Leclerc
de la Champmeslé
19
Pl de
la Calende
R du Général Leclerc
R du Bac

18
P
R du Général Leclerc
R Lelieur
R des Tonneliers
12
2
de la Savonnerie
R Grand Pont
R de la Tour de Beure
Pl de la
Haute-Vieille
Tour
Pl du
Gaillardbois
Les
Halles
R St-Denis
R de Québec

Quai du Havre
Quai de la Bourse
9
5
Voie sur Berge
Quai Pierre Corneille
26
Pl de la
République
Quai de

Pont
Jeanne
d'Arc
Quai Cavelier de la Salle
R des Docks
R P Chirol
Joffre-
Mutualité
9 **16** **21**
Av / Cartier
La Seine
Pont
Boieldieu
Quai Jean Moulin
Quai St-Sever
Pont
Corneille
17
ILE
LACRO

from there evocative little rue Damiette heads towards St-Ouen church. For a break or a meal in this quarter, there are tempting outdoor tables of brasseries and restaurants along the edges of place de la Cathédrale.

Cathédrale Notre Dame

ⓘ *Place de la Cathédrale, cathedrale-rouen. net. Apr-Oct: Sun (and religious festivals) 0800-1800, Mon 1400-1900, Tue-Sat 0900-1900. Nov-Mar: Sun (and religious festivals) 1400-1800, Mon-Sat 0900-1200, 1400-1800. Closed to visitors during services, and on 1 Jan, 1 May, 1-3 Oct, 8-12 Oct, 15-19 Oct, 11 Nov. Free.*

Its two towers rising high over the Old Quarter, Rouen's cathedral is considered one of the most beautiful examples of Gothic craftsmanship in Europe. Its exuberant architecture is the focal point of the city and provides a living link between today's city and its ancient past.

Immense damage was done to the cathedral during the Second World War and the repair work and restoration continue to this day, but it remains an awesome spectacle. Stand on the edge of place de la Cathédrale, facing the main west front, and you are more or less on the spot where Impressionist artist Claude Monet set up his easel. He painted this ornate façade 28 times. Each of those pictures is today worth tens of millions of dollars, pounds or euros – which is why the city of Rouen itself owns just one of them!

The original church on this site was built in AD 393, and marked the beginning of Rouen's rise to prominence as an ecclesiastical centre. In AD 488 the first cathedral was built here, and grew in successive centuries. By the ninth century, the city and its cathedral made a fine target for Viking raiders, who began a 50-year process of destruction and theft. However, when Rollo became the first duke of the new Duchy of Normandy, he converted to Christianity and ordered the rebuilding of all damaged churches. The first Norman cathedral on the site – in the Romanesque style they made their own – dates from about AD 1000 and partly survives as the crypt of the present cathedral.

Following a fire in 1200, the cathedral was entirely rebuilt, with great success, in the new Gothic style. For the next 400 years it was added to and enhanced as the Gothic period evolved. For example, one of the towers, Tour St Romain, is partly 12th-century early Gothic and embellished with much later sculpture, while the other tower, oddly called the Tour de Beurre, was built 300 years later in a more elaborate style and topped with a Flamboyant crown. It is explained that the Tour de Beurre (literally 'tower of butter') gets its name from having been funded by selling dispensations to those who did not wish to give up butter during Lent. It's easy to see though that this tower's stone is actually a creamier colour than the rest.

Inside, the cathedral has an immense sense of light and space. There are important Gothic and Renaissance tombs, notably that of Rollo, first duke of Normandy, and another containing the heart of Richard the Lionheart. The beautiful stained-glass windows, dating from the 13th to the 16th centuries, survived the war by being removed and put into safe keeping.

Eglise St-Maclou

ⓘ *Place Barthélemy. Apr-Oct Sat-Sun 1000-1200 and 1400-1800; Nov-Mar Sat-Sun 1000-1200 and 1400-1730; closed the rest of the week, and 25 Dec and 1 Jan. Free.*

It could do with a clean, and the pigeons are a deterrent, but for all that this magnificent 15th-century church is a beautiful sight with its white, Late Flamboyant Gothic stonework and fine porch with imposing portals. The central tympanum shows the Last Judgement, while rich carving on the 16th-century wooden doors depicts the Good Shepherd, the Baptism of Christ and the Virgin Mary. The interior is more simple, but elegant, with a Flamboyant Gothic staircase climbing to a Renaissance organ loft.

Aître de St-Maclou

ⓘ *186 rue Martainville. Mon-Fri 0800-2000 (1900 in winter), Sat-Sun and festivals 0900-1200, 1400-1900. Free.*

This lovely large enclosed courtyard of immaculate timbered buildings, today so enchanting, was originally a communal plague pit dating back to the Black Death. On the same theme, it subsequently served as an ossuary. Skulls and bones and gravediggers' tools carved into the wooden beams hint at its unsettling past. In complete contrast, it now the home of a school of fine arts.

Abbatiale St-Ouen

ⓘ *Place du Général de Gaulle. Daily (except Mon and Fri) 1000-1200 and 1400-1800 (1700 in winter). Free.*

Graceful and exuberant, this huge 134-m-long church is a superb example of Gothic architecture. It's made of fine white stone, rather blackened outside but beautiful within, and with lovely 14th-century stained-glass windows. A former church on the site was originally built to house the tomb of seventh-century Bishop Ouen, who had been vitally important in Christianizing the region and founded a great Benedictine Abbey here. His abbey was so often harassed and attacked by Norse raiders that it fell into ruins. The first attempts to recreate it were made by Duke Rollo, but another building in Norman style took its place in 1066. In the 14th century, the abbot had the whole church almost entirely demolished and elegantly rebuilt in Gothic style. Much further work was done in the 15th century, and it was not completed for another 100 years. Even after that time, further additions were made, including the only false note in the building – the artless alterations to the west front in the 19th century. The church has a majestic 19th-century organ made by Aristide Cavaillé-Coll, and one modern stained-glass window by Max Ingrand, installed in 1960.

Gros Horloge and Vieux Marché → *For listings, see pages 32-39.*

Rouen's main square, place du Vieux Marché, is more than the 'old market square' of its name. It is a focal point for the city's emotions and its history, with a religious, a secular and a patriotic role to play. Here are restaurants, bars and entertainment where the Rouennais come for an evening's pleasant relaxation, yet also in this square are memorials to poignant events that took place on this spot hundreds of years ago. In February 1431, Joan of Arc, having turned the fortunes of France in its 100-year war with England, was tried by a French ecclesiastical court and found guilty of heresy. On 30 May she was tied to a stake in this marketplace, and her judges watched as she was executed by fire. Just 24 years later the verdict was reversed and in 1920 she was beatified and declared a patron saint of France.

Rue du Gros Horloge, the most popular sight in Rouen, links place du Vieux Marché to the town's other great square, place de la Cathédrale. Crowded and commercial, but charming, cobbled, lined with old buildings and utterly picturesque, it's the main shopping street and is spanned by the fascinating Gros Horloge, Rouen's most distinctive landmark.

Place du Vieux Marché
Originally the town's medieval marketplace, the square was ingeniously restored in the 1970s and today seems curiously undateable. There is no view across the square as its centre is taken up with the rather unattractive exterior of the modern Joan of Arc church and the small covered market which is part of the same construction. Close to the church a slender modern crucifix, soaring to a height of 20 m, marks the exact place where Joan was tied to the stake and burned while her judges sat and watched. Around the edges are handsome half-timbered buildings with the polish of recent construction. At street level, many of the buildings have been turned into bars and restaurants popular with locals and tourists.

Eglise Ste-Jeanne-d'Arc (St Joan of Arc Church)
ⓘ *Place du Vieux Marché. Daily Apr-Oct 1000-1200 and 1400-1800 (1700 Nov-Mar), closed Fri and Sun morning and during services. Free.*
The middle of Rouen's old market square is dominated by the post-war church, designed by Louis Arretche and dedicated to Joan of Arc. It is ultra-modern with concrete construction, with 400-year-old glass along one side. The sanctification of Joan is itself a modern phenomenon (she was canonized in 1920), and the building serves as powerful statement that the Catholic church is still relevant to the present day. The curious twisted architecture, the interior on a different axis than the exterior, is supposed to be drawn from the shapes of shipping and docks. Certainly the bowed wood and metal ceiling could be reminiscent of the keel of a ship. There is no nave: the church appears to be a meeting hall with rows of pews curved around the altar. The panels of fine 16th-century stained glass, saved from wartime destruction, are the most pleasing aspect of the church.

Gros Horloge

Rue du Gros Horloge, T02 32 08 01 90. Daily except Mon, Apr-Oct 1000-1300 and 1400-1900, Nov-Mar 1400-1800, last admission 1 hr before closing. €6, €3 child/concession.

Rouen's bustling, appealing old thoroughfare, rue du Gros Horloge, gets its name from the mighty clock spanning the street. On this spot in medieval times there was a city gate, Porte Massacre; rising beside it stood a belfry that housed the Gros Horloge. In the 16th century the gate was largely demolished and the clock was moved from the belfry on to the gate's remaining archway, which was reconstructed especially to hold the huge mechanism. Carvings of the Good Shepherd and his flock decorate the archway.

The Gros Horloge itself, gilded and ornate, is a remarkable mechanism, with a clock face on each side so it can be seen whichever way you approach it. One hand revolves around each clock face, showing the hours of the day, while a central panel shows the phases of the moon and the passing of the weeks. It is accurate to this day.

The old belfry still survives, and still tolls the nightly curfew bell at 2100 as it has for over 700 years. A spiral staircase winds to the top, where a balcony (added in the 18th century) gives a thrilling view of the city's rooftops and spires and landmarks. It was from this vantage point that Corot painted *The Seine near Rouen* in about 1830, showing how surprisingly close the countryside came to the city centre at that time.

Palais de Justice (Law Courts) – Parlement de Normandie

Rue aux Juifs. The interior is closed to visitors for security reasons, but ask at the tourist office about guided visits, which are sometimes possible.

In a narrow street parallel to rue du Gros Horloge, just 100 m away, Rouen's law courts occupy a gorgeous early 16th-century complex in white stone so intricately carved that the upper section of the façade appears to be a screen of delicate lace concealing part of the roof. The whole structure is considered one of northern Europe's finest surviving examples of medieval civic architecture. The west wing is the oldest part, being originally a merchants' trading hall completed in 1509. The central building was then begun, first to house the Exchequer of Rouen, and then the Parlement de Normandie (Normandy Parliament) set up by François I. The east wing was added in the 19th century in the same style.

Parts of the building were bombed to smithereens on the night of 18-19 April 1944, and then bombed again on 26 August. When the war was over a huge project began to repair it; the work still continues. On the side and back of the structure some marks of wartime damage have been left in place.

The best spot to appreciate the beauty of the building is right in front of the main central courtyard set back from rue aux Juifs. A vast amount of exuberant and accomplished Gothic and Renaissance sculpture and stonework decorates its exterior, increasing in complexity and profusion as it rises up the façade. A stone staircase leads up to the only part which may sometimes be open to the public (on guided tours with advance booking at the tourist office), the Salle des Procureurs or Salle des Pas Perdus, a huge old courtroom with galleries at each end and an impressive modern panelled roof, 16.5-m wide.

The name of the street comes from this having been the heart of medieval Rouen's principal Jewish neighbourhood until Jews were expelled from France in 1306. Their property and possessions were confiscated and sold at auction by the Exchequer of Rouen in the same year. Jews were readmitted nine years later on payment of a fee, then re-expelled (today there is again a Jewish community in Rouen).

Excavation of the Palais de Justice courtyard in 1976, together with a study of contemporary documents, revealed that part of the Palais de Justice stands upon the remains of a medieval yeshiva (a Jewish religious academy), sections of which are being exposed to view during work on the east wing. Renamed 'La Maison Sublime' by the municipality, the yeshiva ruins are of a substantial three or four-storey Romanesque building dating from about 1100. (Guided tours Tuesday 1500, lamaisonsublime.fr).

Museum Quarter → *For listings, see pages 32-39.*

Between the historic heart of the Old Town and the encircling boulevards de la Marne and de l'Yser to its north is a less picturesque district with a more workaday atmosphere. Here wide residential and commercial avenues cut straight lines towards the railway station and the ring road. They are, however, interspersed with many more ancient backstreets and lanes of 18th-century stone mansions and older half-timbered houses. Just two or three streets north of the main sightseeing area, the huge, purpose-built Musée des Beaux Arts is the focal point of this quiet area of museums. Facing the Musée des Beaux Arts, the spacious park of square Verdrel provides a tree-shaded haven of tranquillity and repose. In the 16th century, this neighbourhood was home to a wealthy Irish community of the merchant class, who built the large St-Patrice church, known today for its wealth of good 16th- and 17th-century stained-glass windows. All around the area are intriguing and unusual museums well worth visiting. On the northern edge of the district, Tour Jeanne d'Arc is a last remnant of Rouen's 13th-century fortifications.

Musée des Beaux Arts (Fine Arts Museum)
ⓘ *Esplanade Marcel-Duchamp (Square Verdrel), disabled access 26 bis rue Jean-Lecanuet, T02 35 71 28 40, rouen-musees.com. Wed-Mon 1000-1800 (South Wing closed 1300-1400), closed during national holidays. €5, €3 concessions, under-26s free.*
This large museum, one of France's premier art collections, contains over 300 works of painting and sculpture from the 15th century up to the modern period, arranged in more than 60 rooms. The galleries devoted to the 15th to 17th centuries are exceptional for Flemish Primitives and Italian Primitives, with superb works by Gérard David and Pietro Perugino, and later, by François Clouet, Paolo Véronèse, Caravaggio, Velasquez, Rubens and many more.

The museum is renowned especially for 19th-century painting. A focal point for visitors is the single example of Monet's paintings of the west façade of Rouen cathedral. There are numerous other outstanding Impressionist works, and views of the Seine appear and reappear in the paintings by Monet, Sisley, Boudin and others. Also on display in this section are works by Ingres, Poussin, Degas, Corot, Millet, and many other great names of early modern art. A good space is devoted to 20th-century art, among which are outstanding pieces by Modigliani, the brothers Duchamp, Dufy and Villon.

Musée de la Céramique (Ceramics Museum)
ⓘ *1 rue Faucon or 94 rue Jeanne d'Arc (square Verdrel), T02 35 07 31 74, rouen-musees.com. Wed-Mon 1000-1300 and 1400-1800, closed during national holidays. €3, €2 concessions, under-26s free.*
Facing the greenery of Square Verdrel, this neighbour of the Musée des Beaux Arts occupies the imposing neo-Classical 17th-century mansion Hôtel d'Hocqueville. Both the house and the museum are interesting. With exceptional rich collections of exquisite porcelain, totalling over 5000 pieces, the museum gives a comprehensive overview of the whole period of Rouen's manufacture of high-quality traditional faience from the mid-16th century up to the 19th century when it went into decline. The work ranges from floor

tiles and tableware and ordinary household objects – beautifully coloured and painted – to precious ornaments and creative curiosities like the Celestial and Terrestrial Globes by Pierre Chapelle, dated 1725. As a comparison, there is also some fine faience ware from Nevers, Lille and Delft, and 100 19th- and 20th-century pieces from Sèvres.

Musée le Secq des Tournelles (Le Secq des Tournelles Museum)
ⓘ *2 rue Jacques Villon (disabled access rue Deshays), T02 35 88 42 92, rouen-musees.com. Wed-Mon 1000-1300 and 1400-1800, closed during national holidays. €3, €2 concessions, under-26s free.*
Behind the Musée des Beaux Arts rises the elaborate Flamboyant spire of Eglise St-Laurent, deconsecrated since the Revolution. Today this 15th-century Gothic church houses the remarkable collection of wrought-iron work assembled during the late 19th century by father and son Henri Le Secq des Tournelles. It has become Europe's leading collection of such workmanship, covering the whole range imaginable of things that could made of wrought iron. Displays include jewellery, hairdressers' and surgeons' tools, a 13th-century screen door, fantastically intricate 15th-century locks, a complete 18th-century stair rail from a château, and fascinating centuries-old inn and shop signs.

Musée des Antiquités (Antiquities Museum)
ⓘ *Entrance through Ste-Marie cloister, 198 rue Beauvoisine, T02 35 98 55 10. museedesantiquites.fr. Closed Mon and national holidays, open Tue-Sat 1330-1730, Sun 1400-1800. €3, €2 concessions, under-18s free.*
Situated inside a former 17th-century monastery, the museum brings together an eclectic assortment of remarkable art, craftsmanship and archaeology. Its great highlight is the Lillebonne Mosaic, uncovered in a town centre garden at Lillebonne (between Rouen and Le Havre). Originally the dining room floor of a Roman villa, the beautifully complete 6-m-square mosaic depicts stag hunting, a sacrifice to Diana and, in the circular central panel, a lustful youth – probably Apollo – seizing a nymph. In another room, the 11th-century Valasse Cross is one of the oldest pieces of Limoges enamel work. Step into the Salle des Tapisseries to see the 15th-century Flemish tapestry Winged Deer, displayed among 16th-century furnishings.

The neighbouring Jesuit school, Lycée Corneille, was renamed in honour of its most distinguished old boy, the 17th-century playwright Pierre Corneille, regarded as the father of French drama. Several other former pupils of the school went on to great renown, including the painter Jean-Baptiste Camille Corot and writers Gustave Flaubert and Guy de Maupassant.

Tour Jeanne d'Arc or Le Donjon (Joan of Arc Tower)
ⓘ *Rue du Donjon, but entrance is round the corner in rue Bouvreuil, T02 35 98 16 21. Closed Tue and national holidays, open Mon-Sat (except Tue) 1000-1200 and 1400-1800, Sun 1400-1830, closes 1 hr earlier Oct-Mar. €1.50, no concessions, under-18s free.*
This sturdy round tower under its conical roof is a last remnant of Rouen's medieval fortifications. It looks a little out of place standing alone among modern buildings close to a main road near the station. Originally, it was part of a massive 13th-century castle, long since demolished leaving no other trace. The donjon is a dauntingly solid structure – the walls are 4 m thick. Despite the name, it has little or nothing to do with Joan of Arc. She was imprisoned not here, but in another tower, which no longer exists. However it is possible that this was the place to which she was brought on 9 May 1431, to be threatened with torture and shown the instruments that would be used on her if she did not confess to heresy (she did in fact confess).

Today the tower, with steps spiralling all the way to the top, is used as a small museum, with displays about Joan of Arc's trial, and about the history of the castle that once stood here.

Rouen to Lyons → *For listings, see pages 32-39.*

Around Rouen, in either direction along the chalky cliffs and wooded banks of the Seine, are dozens of interesting and attractive places to visit. Among them are forests, waterfront villages, great ruins dating back to the Duchy of Normandy and majestic vistas.

For a single excursion that takes in all these things, drive out of the city to **Lyons-la-Forêt**, a short drive northeast of Rouen. From there make your way to Les Andelys on the Seine, and turn along the river's north bank back towards Rouen. Avoiding the major roads beside the river, the easiest exit from Rouen's city centre is rue d'Amiens, a turning off the main road rue de la République between the cathedral and the church of St-Ouen. Rue d'Amiens continues straight out of the city centre, passes beneath N28 and becomes Route de Lyons-la-Forêt. Through the city fringes, follow signs to Lyons-la-Forêt. At St Léger-du-Bourg-Denis, stay on D42 heading towards Lyons. Forest soon appears on the horizon, and the road continues towards woodlands, entering into countryside of dense forest and rustic farmland.

Nestling in a hollow in the middle of the forest, Lyons-la-Forêt is a quiet picture-postcard village of heavily timbered traditional Normandy houses gathered around a splendid old covered market. The Anglo-Norman King Henry I of England died here in 1135 after a notorious 'surfeit of lampreys', which he had eaten the previous night at the Cistercian monastery of Mortemer, 4 km away.

The ruins of Mortemer (see page 64), off the road to Les Andelys, make an enjoyable detour as you head out of Lyons-la-Forêt on D2. The third turning on the left leads to a narrow lane which runs steeply down to the ruins in the valley of the Fouillebroc stream, by a lake.

Back on D2, leave the woodlands for the high open fields of the Caux country towards the double spires of **Ecouis**. Pause when you reach the village (on the crossroads of the D2 and major road D6014) to have a closer look at this impressive church, the Collégiale Notre Dame de l'Assomption, in place du Cloître.

Inside, there is good 14th-century wood-carving and sculpture. Drive across open, rolling countryside of farmland on narrow D2, changing to D1 after Fresne-de-l'Archevêque and descending into Le Grand Andely.

Le Grand Andely and riverside Le Petit Andely together make up the town of **Les Andelys** (see page 70) which, straddling a tributary called the Gambon, rises from the River Seine. The most picturesque corners are in Le Petit Andely, close to the Seine, with views of the Seine valley's chalky cliff curving away into the distance. High on a cliff top overlooking the town stands the Château Gaillard (see page 70), Richard the Lionheart's daunting white castle built to defend the Seine valley from the French.

Leave Le Petit Andely on D313, signposted to Pont St-Pierre. After 3 km, turn left to stay on D313. This road, at first mainly running between the broad river and the white cliffs, becomes wooded until the river disappears from view. Still the scene remains typical of the Seine valley: calm, rural, bathed in light. At Muids, follow D313 as it turns away from the river's edge, rejoining it at Andé. Once more follow the river road round to Amfreville and La Côte des Deux Amants, from which there is a good view of the Seine and its Amfreville locks.

Cross the River Andelle through Romilly-sur-Andelle to take D126. This road meets the major road N14 (or D6014) at Boos. Here turn towards Rouen and continue, through some unappealing suburbs, back into the city centre.

Rouen listings

For hotel and restaurant price codes and other relevant information, see pages 10-14.

🛏 Where to stay

Stay outside the city centre if you want to find some of the most inexpensive accommodation. There are budget hotels on the south side of the Seine, see page 34.

Cathedral Quarter *p23, map 24*
€€€ Mercure Centre Cathédrale, rue Croix de Fer, T02 35 52 69 52, mercure.com. Modern and comfortable, with simple, elegant uncluttered decor and rooms with a literary theme including pictures of books and portraits of writers. Some rooms are on the small side, while others are generously proportioned. The car park is cramped and difficult to use, but is nevertheless a welcome addition here on the edge of the pedestrian zone. Service is professional, willing and helpful. The greatest attraction here is the location, in the heart of Old Rouen almost next door to the cathedral.
€€ Le Cardinal, 1 place de la Cathédrale, T02 35 70 24 42, cardinal-hotel.fr. If location is everything, this is hard to beat. With rather cramped but clean and adequately equipped rooms in attractive pastel shades, this small and friendly family-run hotel might be an unremarkable 2-star (although it does offer free Wi-Fi) but it stands out for its excellent position facing the cathedral. It's almost impossible to reach by car, though; you'll have to park in a nearby car park and walk to the hotel.
€€-€ Hôtel des Carmes, place des Carmes, T02 35 71 92 31, hoteldescarmes. com. An unusual, attractive and utterly charming small hotel in a pleasant post-war square between Rouen's cathedral and St-Ouen church. The Carmes has an arty, eccentric feel with pictures everywhere, and simple decor varying from pleasing warm hues to more striking colour combinations. Adequately comfortable little rooms (with free Wi-Fi) have good bathrooms, and here and there are quirkier touches, like a cloud-painted ceiling. The owners speak English and are helpful and considerate. Guests pay a reduced rate at a nearby car park.

Gros Horloge and Vieux Marché
p27, map p24
€€€€ Hôtel de Bourgtheroulde, 15 place de la Pucelle, T02 35 14 50 50, hoteldebourgtheroulde.com. Dating back to 1499, this magnificent late-Gothic and Renaissance mansion (the name is pronounced 'boor-troode') is the city's finest private house of the period. It was a lucky survival after much of its surrounding neighbourhood was destroyed in 1944. Controversially for some Rouennais, it has been transformed into a 4-star luxury hotel, part of the **Marriot Autograph** collection, with its own gastronomic restaurant and brasserie, and a sumptuous spa.
€€€ Hôtel du Vieux Marché, rue du Vieux Palais, T02 35 71 00 88, hotel-vieuxmarche.com. The location in a pedestrian street just off place du Vieux Marché is the strong point of this small, very much modernized traditional **Best Western** hotel within easy walking distance of the sights of Old Rouen. The hotel has its own small pay-to-use car park, a great boon in this quarter. The rooms are comfortable, if some on the small side, in dark-red tones with low lighting. Room rates may be heavily discounted if they are booked online.
€€ Le Dandy, bis rue Cauchoise, T02 35 07 32 00, hotels-rouen.net. With some surprisingly grand Louis Quinze furnishings in an otherwise contemporary setting, this friendly and welcoming small hotel has cosy, modernized rooms. It is well placed in a pedestrian street of small shops and eateries that leads to place du Vieux Marché,

frequented more by locals than tourists. In the front rooms there may be a little noise from local bars. Rooms at the rear are quieter.

Museum Quarter *p29, map p24*
€ Hôtel Morand, rue Morand, T02 35 71 46 07, morandhotel.com. This is a basic, traditional, family-run hotel, not without charm, on a street corner in a fairly low-key mainly residential part of town. Rooms are a decent size, if perhaps in need of some modernization, and the owners are friendly and helpful. Located just north of the Musée des Beaux Arts and the green square Verdrel, it's outside the busiest part of the tourist area, yet within easy reach of everything.

Elsewhere *map p24*
Near stations
€€€ Hôtel Ermitage Bouquet, 58 rue Bouquet, T02 32 12 30 40, hotel-ermitage bouquet.com. This is a pleasant, well-equipped, comfortable hotel in a quiet spot outside the city's historic area. A 19th-century brick building, unusually it's both a member of the upmarket **Châteaux et Hôtels de France** and the cosier, traditional, family-run **Logis de France**. It has useful off-street parking and free Wi-Fi. Decor is simple and uncluttered, with plenty of stylish touches including polished wooden floors and chandeliers. The rooms and bathrooms are modern and well equipped, the breakfast good, and staff helpful. It's north of the railway station, on a steep hill, about 15 mins' walk to the sights of Old Rouen.
€€ Hôtel de Dieppe, Bernard Tissot, T02 35 71 96 00, hotel-dieppe.fr. This is a simple, modest, independent hotel right across the road from the railway station. With thoroughly French provincial character, while parts of the hotel may seem in urgent need of modernization, it is better known in the town for its good traditional restaurant – the speciality of the house is the classic local dish, *canard à la rouennaise* (Rouen duck).

€ Hôtel Andersen, rue Pouchet, T02 35 71 88 51, hotelandersen.com. Close to the railway station, in a not very appealing backstreet but away from the worst of the traffic noise, the white façade of this basic hotel for low-budget travellers is appealing. The interior is welcoming, with light, pleasant decoration. The public areas have more charm than the bedrooms, which are not particularly large, and some fixtures and fittings seem to need improvement. There's a decent traditional breakfast.
€ Hôtel Astrid, place Bernard Tissot/rue Jeanne d'Arc, T02 35 71 75 88, hotel-astrid.fr. This is a very simple, basic, traditional hotel in a corner position right across from the railway station. It can be noisy, both from the street and from neighbouring bedrooms. Rooms are small and bathrooms poky, but for anyone looking to keep expenses down, not fussy about comforts and/or travelling by train, it's ideal. Staff are amiable and helpful and a modest breakfast is available. The sights of Old Rouen are easily reached by bus or on foot.

Riverside North Bank
€€€ Mercure Champ de Mars, av Aristide Briand, T02 35 52 42 32, hotel-rouen-centre. com. Arguably the best, or at least smartest, of Rouen's hotels, this **Mercure** is on a busy main road in a riverside setting east of Old Rouen. Behind the hotel is the pleasant Esplanade Champs de Mars. Catering mainly to the business market, with a strongly corporate feel, it's comfortable and well equipped with plush and warm decor, but without being especially luxurious. There's a pub-like piano bar and a good restaurant, sometimes with live jazz.
€€€ Suitehôtel Rouen Normandie, Îlot Pasteur, Quai de Boisguilbert, T02 32 10 58 68, suite-hotel.com. On a rather bleak busy riverside roadway on the north bank of the Seine, about 1.5 km from the sights of Old Rouen, this functional modern white block adorned with balconies offers pleasant,

spacious cleverly designed accommodation arranged more like a simple apartment (complete with a small cooking area) rather than a classic hotel room. Decor in the rooms and in the public areas is bright and contemporary, staff are helpful and there is an underground car park.

€€-€ Hôtel de Paris, 14 rue de la Champmeslé, T02 35 70 09 26, hotel-paris.fr. A classic small family-run hotel of the old style, just off the Seine waterfront, the Paris is a few minutes' stroll from all the sights of Old Rouen. The welcome is friendly and professional, and the hotel appears clean and well kept. There's a decent continental breakfast buffet, and it's useful that the hotel has its own car park. Rooms are simply and pleasantly decorated, unpretentious, not large but very adequately equipped.

€ Hôtel Arts et Seine, 6 rue St-Etienne des Tonneliers, T02 35 88 11 44, artsetseine. com. South of the cathedral, a block away from the Seine riverside, this hotel is in a post-war commercial area which is perhaps not Rouen's prettiest neighbourhood, but is just a few minutes' walk to all the main sights. Outwardly not very appealing, this is a friendly, helpful and well managed family-run hotel, with clean, comfortable rooms, furnished in smart, modern, uncluttered style. Free Wi-Fi. There is sometimes noise at night from nearby bars.

€ Ibis Rouen Champ de Mars, av Aristide Briand, T02 35 08 12 11, rouen-centre-hotel. fr. An inexpensive modern budget chain hotel, this Ibis stands beside a busy main riverside highway east of Old Rouen. It's about 15 mins' walk to the main sights. Rooms have a pleasing, comfortable simplicity. Behind the hotel, the Esplanade Champs de Mars provides a pleasant prospect. The hotel is an efficient cheap option for both business and leisure travellers, and also has its own car park.

South of the Seine
€€ Rouen Saint Sever, place de l'Eglise St-Sever, T02 35 62 81 82,

simplyhotelsfrance.com. If you're looking to economize, and are prepared to go without a few creature comforts, this former budget chain hotel beside a commercial centre south of the Seine could be a good choice. The small, functional rooms, each with a little bathroom tacked on, are clean and adequate and the beds are comfortable. Tourists do stay here, but the focus seems to be on one-night business stays and group bookings.

€ Ibis Rouen Centre Rive Gauche, rue Amiral Cécille, T02 35 63 27 27, ibishotel. com. This reliable, low-budget hotel is opposite a commercial centre about 1 km from Old Rouen. A good cheap option, it's clean, and comfortable. It offers Wi-Fi and also has a car park.

€ Premiere Classe Rouen Petit Quevilly, av Jean Jaurès, T02 35 72 02 22, premiere-classe-rouen-ouest-petit-quevilly.fr. This budget chain hotel is a plain and simple low-rise on a main road (D3) on the south side of the Seine, about 3 km from Old Rouen. A tram into town passes in front of the door. On offer are small, clean and modern rooms, with minimal service. The location is convenient for getting to town, and there's a basic breakfast to see you on your way.

Suburbs
€ Auberge de Jeunesse, de Darnetal, fuaj.org/rouen. Open 24 hrs a day, 7 days a week. Housed in a former 18th-century dye manufacturers', right on the banks of the River Robec, northeast of the city centre, Rouen's brand-new, top-of-the-range youth hostel, due to open in 2010, is on a TEOR bus route with access to the central area.

Restaurants

Cathedral Quarter *p23, map 24*
€€ Brasserie Paul, place de la Cathédrale, T02 35 71 86 07. Daily 1200-1500 and approximately 1930-2300. 100 years old, full of classic pre-war touches like art

deco lamps and polished wood, Brasserie Paul claims to be the longest established brasserie in Rouen and is wonderfully positioned beside the cathedral. Sit under pink parasols and choose from menus of French and Normandy favourites – steaks, *tête de veau*, *andouillette*, *escargots* and fine local cheeses, all at reasonable prices.

€ A La Table Gourmande, 25 rue des Bonnetiers, T02 35 71 87 06. Daily 0730-2130. This cheerful brasserie with indoor and outdoor tables near the cathedral is open all day from breakfast to dinner. There's orange and white decor and a café ambience, but decent set menus for lunch and dinner, offering classic French cooking at modest prices.

€ Brasserie de la Flèche, 12 place de la Calende, T02 35 71 95 61. Open all day. There's a green and white colour scheme at this warm and friendly café-bar on the corner of a square right next to the cathedral. Enjoy inexpensive three-course set menus of simple cooking, served out of doors or inside at tables laid with gingham cloths.

Gros Horloge and Vieux Marché
p27, map p24

€€€ La Couronne, 31 place du Vieux Marché, T02 35 71 40 90, lacouronne.com.fr. Daily 1200-1430 and 1900-2230. A famous name and acclaimed as 'the oldest auberge in France', this picturesque flower and flag-decked Vieux Marché landmark has a dark timber façade, plenty of wood beams, plush fabrics, warm lighting and cosy ambience. Classic Norman cooking is served, including a *véritable*, and pricey, *canard à la Rouennaise à la presse*.

€€€ Les Nymphéas, 7/9 rue de la Pie, T02 35 89 26 69, lesnympheas-rouen.com. Tue-Sat 1200-1400 and 1930-2145, closed Sun and Mon (except national holidays). Among the top names for Old Rouen gourmets, this traditional place in Old Rouen is sumptuously furnished, with white napery, flowers and upholstered chairs. It's on 2 floors of a half-timbered old house in its

own courtyard off the Vieux Marché. Menu specialities are hearty French and Norman fare, such as *canard à la rouennaise* and *civet de homard au Sauternes*.

€€€-€€ Origine, 26 Rampe Cauchoise, T02 35 70 95 52, restaurant-origine.com. Mon-Fri 1215-1415, 1915-2200. Venture a few paces outside the tourist zone, following traffic-free rue Cauchoise away from the Vieux Marché, and across busy place Cauchoise. Just beyond, this elegant, contemporary and comfortable Michelin-starred restaurant offers a single set menu of refined and imaginative French cuisine at each mealtime. Choose anything from a bargain 2-course lunch up to a gastronomic 6-courses. Pleasing service and presentation. Excellent cheeses, and good Calvados to finish.

€€ Gill Côté Bistro, 14 place du Vieux Marché, T02 35 89 88 72, gill.fr/fr/bistro.php. Daily 1200-1500 and 1930-2300. In addition to his successful Michelin-starred riverside restaurant (see page 37), chef Gilles Tournadre also runs this more informal, low-key alternative on what is unfortunately the least attractive corner of the Vieux Marché. However, the bistro itself is contemporary, stylish and smart, with attractive woods and dark green hues. There's Gilles' same emphasis on local ingredients, but with dishes inspired by all of France and beyond, such as *bœuf bourguignon* with fresh pasta.

€€ Minute et Mijoté, 58 rue de Fontenelle, T02 32 08 40 00. http://minutemijote.canal blog.com. Mon-Sat 1200-1400 and 1945-2200, closed part of Aug. In brasserie-style premises with tables standing among greenery on the pavement, this restaurant not far from place du Vieux Marché serves well-prepared French dishes, both local and from other regions, on monthly changing menus.

€€-€ Le Maupassant, 39 place du Vieux Marché, T02 35 07 56 90, le-maupassant-rouen.fr. Daily 1200-1400 and 1900-2230. Busy and touristy, of course, as it is on the Vieux Marché, on a pedestrian section, facing the Ste-Jeanne-d'Arc church. Service is generally amiable, and the cooking competent and good value for money. There are French classics on the menu, and some surprises, such as duck crumble with chorizo. Finish with their *moelleux au chocolat*.

€ Bistrot des Hallettes, 43 place du Vieux Marché, T02 35 71 05 06, bistrot-hallettes. fr. Tue-Sat 1200-1430 and 1930-2230. With plenty of red plush and walls of bare brick, the interior of this restaurant has a warm informality. Outside, there's plenty of seating at tables on the Vieux Marché cobbles. Food and wine is generous and hearty, with fine steaks, kidneys, snails and *andouillette*.

€ Le Florian, 11 rue de Crosne, T02 35 07 47 17. Mon-Sat 1200-1400 and 1900-2300. *Trompe l'œil* decorates the upper floors of this pizzeria facing into place du Vieux Marché, a boon if you want a good, simple meal at a low price. Inside, the restaurant is in an atmospheric old vaulted basement with tiled floors, arched white ceilings, and walls of stone blocks decorated with intriguing Venetian masks.

€ Maison Hardy, 22 place du Vieux Marché, T02 35 71 81 55. Mon-Sat lunchtime only. A charcuterie with sausages and prepared meats, the shop also has a little restaurant serving good-value set lunches.

Cafés and bars

L'Euro, 41 place du Vieux Marché, T02 35 07 55 66. Daily 1500-0200. A spacious array of outdoor café tables look on to place du Vieux Marché, while inside this historic half-timbered corner building are three different bars: on the ground floor a cocktail/lounge bar ambience; on the first floor a bar serving French wines with charcuterie and cheeses; and on the top floor a livelier show bar and disco.

Le Vicomte, 70 rue de la Vicomte, T02 35 71 24 11. Daily 1800-0200. There's a lot going on in this popular 4-storey bar, with cocktails and DJ on the ground level, live music and performers on the 1st floor, a billiard room upstairs, and private events room.

Museum Quarter *p29, map p24*

€€€ Les Petits Parapluies, 46 rue Bourg l'Abbé/place de la Rougemare, T02 35 88 55 26. Tue-Sun approx 1200-1345 and approx 1930-2200, closed Sat lunch and Sun dinner. This leading Rouen restaurant specializes in inventive French cooking with local inspiration, such as *foie gras* cooked in cider, with apple and red onion crumble. It is sited in a fine half-timbered building where once umbrellas were made. Interiors are sumptuously elegant and stylish, with beamed ceilings, and the food beautifully presented.

€ Brasserie Gilden, 35 rue Jean Lecanuet, T02 35 08 97 12. 0900-2000 (2400 on Fri and Sat), closed Sun. With plenty of space indoors and tables in the square outside as well, this large corner brasserie by the **Musée des Beaux Arts** offers of classic brasserie fare, as well as pizzas and a salad buffet.

Cafés and bars

Bar de la Crosse, 53 rue de l'Hôpital, T02 35 70 16 18. Tue-Sat 1000-2200. This friendly café-bar provides a welcome pause on a traffic-free street that runs from St-Ouen church towards the **Musée des Beaux Arts**.

Le Diplomate, 10 place Foch, T02 35 71 10 80. Daily, all day. This unassuming modern little bar with a few pavement tables, across the road from the back of the Law Courts (the former Parlement de Normandie), has a bright and colourful interior. It also serves a wide choice of inexpensive set menus of traditional French brasserie fare at lunchtime.

Elsewhere *map p24*
Near stations

Le Métropole, 111 rue Jeanne d'Arc, T02 71 58 56. Mon-Fri 0730-1930, Sat 0800-1300. Perched on a narrow street corner, this 1930s art deco brasserie was the haunt of Jean-Paul Sartre and Simone de Beauvoir. Relaxed and pleasant inside, with Wi-Fi, drinks, snacks and a set *formule* at lunchtime.

Riverside North Bank

€€€ Gill, 8-9 quai de la Bourse, T02 35 71 16 14, gill.fr. Tue-Sat 1200-1345 and 1930-2145, closed 2 weeks in Apr, most of Aug, and Christmas and New Year. The gastronomic restaurant of renowned chef Gilles Tournadre, on the north bank of the River Seine, is considered the supreme dining experience in Rouen. With 2 Michelin stars, it has a refined simplicity and elegance in design and in cuisine. Among the menu highlights there is *pigeon à la Rouennaise*, which is a twist on the more traditional duckling *à la Rouennaise*. See also **Gill Côté Bistro**, page 35.

€€ Le 37, 37 rue des Tonneliers, T02 35 70 56 65. Tue-Sat 1200-1345 and 1930-2145. Chic and cheerful in long, narrow premises with a bistro feel, this informal lavender-tinted restaurant offers rapid service, set menus and excellent French cuisine. Dishes chalked up on a daily blackboard. Finish with the exquisite *fondant au chocolat*, if it's on.

€ Le Tyrol, 36-38 rue de la Champmeslé, T02 35 71 14 32. Mon-Fri 0700-1930, Sat 0830-1900. Open all day for drinks and snacks, with inexpensive set menus at mealtimes, this bright pavement café is just outside the main tourist zone, in the shopping area between Old Rouen and the river.

€ Tex Mex L'Equateur, 5-7 rue du Bac, T02 35 71 22 16. Tue-Sat 1145-1400 and 1900-2300 (Fri and Sat 2400). This bar and restaurant on the Seine north bank is intent on enjoying everything Mexican, from music to drinks to food to upbeat atmosphere. Lunchtime menus are cheap and cheerful.

South of the Seine

€€€ Les Capucines, 16-18 rue Jean Macé, T02 35 72 62 34, bus no 6 from République in the city centre stops at place des Chartreux in Le Petit Quevilly. Tue-Sun 1200-1400 and 1945-2115, closed Sat lunch and Sun dinner and 3 weeks in Aug. This solid, reliable gastronomic address occupies a redbrick house in a residential street in the Le Petit Quevilly area south of the river.

Decor is stylish and traditional with calm, restful tones, with a pretty terrace outside. Popular with business travellers, it's been in the same family for 3 generations. Dishes imaginatively combine Norman flavours with classic French cuisine.

🍷 Bars and clubs

Rouen *p22, map p24*

Throughout the summer, dozens of city centre bars stay open till late, and many have DJs or live music. In the winter months, it's much quieter. The more hectic nightlife is focused around place du Vieux Marché, and between there and the quays of the River Seine. **Irish Pub Yesterday** (rue Moulinet), eclectic **Shari Vari** (51 rue St-Nicolas) and slick **L'Euro** (see page 36) are popular late bars in the city centre. Clubbers can get into a Latin American mood at **La Luna** (26 rue St-Etienne-des-Tonneliers).

🎭 Entertainment

Rouen *p22, map p24*
Music

Opéra de Rouen, 7 rue du Docteur-Rambert/Place des Arts, quai de la Bourse, T02 35 98 74 78 (tickets), operaderouen.com. Rouen's highly regarded **Opéra de Rouen** and Théâtre des Arts, set back from the busy Seine quayside closest to Old Rouen, stages an immense range of high-quality dance, opera and music performances, and a very full programme of classical concerts. Modern dance is frequently featured, with the most prestigious modern dance companies from France and around the world.

Zenith, Av des Canadiens, zenith-de-rouen. com, take bus no 7 to Zénith/Parc Expo terminus. The huge Zenith auditorium stages major rock, pop and other concerts, as well as shows for children and family entertainment. Many of the artists are better known in France than abroad, but some big names also perform here – check what's on during your visit.

Rouen *p22, map p24*

Art and antiques

Chasset Patrick, 12 rue de la Croix de Fer, T02 35 70 59 97. Mon 1430-1900, Tue-Sat 1030-1900. Contains Dinky toys, china, glass and other collectable items.

Faïences Saint-Romain, 56 rue St-Romain, T02 35 07 12 30, faiences-rouen.com. Phone to check opening hours. Makes and sells hand-made ceramic or faience to order.

Faïencerie Augy, 26 rue St Romain, T02 35 88 77 47, fayencerie-augy.com. Tue-Sat 0900-1900. Sells its newly minted traditional-style faience-ware.

Galerie l'Astrée, 10 and 23 rue Damiette, T02 35 70 42 77. Mon 1400-1900, Tue-Sat 1000-1200 and 1400-1900. Astrée have several shops between the cathedral and St-Ouen.

Les Beaux Jours, 24 rue St-Nicolas, T02 35 15 53 24. Tue-Sat 1000-1230 and 1400-1900. Dolls, teddy bears and other toys make an appearance.

Clothing and accessories

Galeries Lafayette, 25 rue Grand-Pont, T02 35 71 70 53, galerieslafayette.com/magasin-rouen. Mon-Sat 0900-1930 (Sat open till 2000). For the latest French fashions and other stylish products.

Hermès, 11 rue du Change, T02 35 71 17 58. Mon 1400-1900, Tue-Sat 1000-1230 and 1400-1900. Women's luxury accessories store, with exceptionally beautiful silk headscarves.

Tant Qu'il y Aura des Hommes, 77 rue St Nicolas, T02 35 70 04 17. Mon 1500-1930, Tue-Thu 1000-1300 and 1430-1930, Fri-Sat 1000-1930. A French chain with stylish, good quality clothes and accessories.

Food and drink

Caves Bérigny, 7 rue Rollon, T02 35 07 57 54. Tue-Sat 0930-1230 and 1430-1930, Sun 1000-1300. This fine wine specialist is also a good place to browse a wide choice of Calvados.

Chocolatier Auzou, 163 rue du Gros Horloge, T02 35 70 59 31. Mon 1415-1915, Tue-Sat 0930-1930, Sun 0930-1300. One of the best-known chocolate makers in town. Sample their local specialities, such as *Larmes de Jeanne d'Arc*, which are almond and nougatine covered with chocolate. A few doors along, they have another shop (Tue-Fri 1030-1900; Sat 0930-1915), devoted to Auzou's other speciality – the most delicious *macarons*.

Comtesse du Barry, 4 rue Rollon, T02 35 07 53 35. Tue-Sat 0900-1300 and 1400-1930. This gourmet boutique chain, right beside place du Vieux Marché, has shelves of preserves, caviar, foie gras, fine wines and more.

La Chocolatière, 18 rue Guillaume le Conquérant, T02 35 71 00 79. Daily 0800-1930. An emporium of chocolate with a café as well as a shop, specializing in pralines.

La Fromagerie du Vieux Marché, 18 rue Rollon, T02 35 71 11 00. Tue-Fri 0900-1245 and 1500-1930, Sat 0900-1900, Sun 0900-1245. Among the diverse array of smart shops in this busy street, is this rather unexpected boutique of a master cheese maker with a fine selection.

Household

Tout pour la Pâtisserie, 56 rue Jeanne d'Arc, T02 35 71 48 32. Mon 1400-1900, Tue-Sat 0900-1200 and 1400-1900. In a town with many kitchenware specialists, here's one with a range of high-quality utensils, specializing in cake and pastry-making.

⚘ What to do

Rouen *p22, map p24*

Cycling

Cy'clic, T08 00 08 78 00, rouen.fr/cyclic. Take advantage of the city's Cy'clic scheme. The 250 help-yourself rental bikes are available at 20 pick-up points around the centre. Insert your credit card and PIN to pick up a bike. It's free for the first 30 mins (long enough to go almost anywhere in town).

You pay €1 for the next 30 mins, €2 for the 30 mins after that. Charges rack up if you keep a bike longer than 1½ hrs.

Walking
Contact the Office de Tourisme de Rouen (Rouen Tourist Office), see page 23, for details and tickets for their varied programme of all-year-round guided walking tours, *Laissez-vous conter Rouen*. Or tour Old Rouen on your own using an audio guide available from the tourist office.

Directory

Rouen *p22, map p24*
Medical services Hospital CHU (Centre Hospitalier Universitaire de Rouen, Hôpital Charles-Nicolle, 1 rue Germont, T02 32 88 89 90, www3.chu-rouen.fr), is the city's large modern hospital. **Pharmacy** There are 18 pharmacies in the city centre, for example, in rue Jeanne d'Arc and rue du Gros-Horloge. One example is Pharmacie de la République (21 rue République, T02 35 70 61 11).

Contents

Footprint features

Upper Normandy

Dieppe

Dieppe's old town lies on a narrow spit of land between the lively, crowded, picturesque harbour with its quaysides on one side, and the 2-km-long pebble beach backed by greensward on the other. Agreeable, traffic-free Grand'Rue, reaching from restaurant-lined Quai Henri IV to place du Puits Salé, is the heart of the old town, and here Dieppe's colourful Saturday morning market is held. Originally an 11th-century Viking port – the name comes from the Norse word for 'deep' – Dieppe became one of the busiest sea ports in France. The imposing Château, overlooking the beach on lofty cliffs behind the town, is a remnant of medieval fortifications. In the 16th century Dieppe was home to Jehan Ango's notorious privateer fleet of 100 ships, but even then it had a recreational quality, and was among the first places in Europe to attract 'tourists'. Henry III visited the town in 1578 to bathe in the sea, laying the foundation of its later reputation. Visits for the same purpose by Queen Hortense of Holland, in 1813, and the influential young Duchess of Berry, every year from 1824 to 1830, gave it the seal of approval for European royalty and high society throughout the 19th century. In the early 20th, it took on a more raffish air. Many artists and writers took up residence, and a community of some 3000 wealthy British expats settled here. No longer so glamorous or fashionable, the town remains lively and attractive, and still attracts crowds of Parisian weekenders.

Arriving in Dieppe

Getting there
Bus station ⓘ *Blvd Clémenceau, T02 35 06 69 33.*

Train station ⓘ *Blvd Clémenceau, T02 35 06 69 33.* For details of regional and national rail services, see page 8.

Getting around
The docks, beach, and town centre of Dieppe all make up a small area that can be crossed on foot in about 20 minutes. For journeys further afield, the greater urban area of Dieppe and its five surrounding suburban villages (Arques-la-Bataille, Hautot-sur-Mer, Martin-Eglise, Rouxmesnil-Bouteilles and St-Aubin-sur-Scie) can all be reached on town buses run by **Stradibus**. The two principal stops in the town centre are the railways station and Pont Ango, between which there are buses every few minutes. A single journey costs €1. A carnet of 10 tickets costs €8.60. Information from **Espace Stradibus** ⓘ *56 quai Duquesne, T02 32 14 03 03, infotransports.free.fr/reseaux/dieppe/informations.htm (Mon-Fri 0800-1200 and 1330-1830, Sat 0900-1200).*

Tourist information
There is a **tourist information office** ⓘ *Pont Jehan Ango, T02-32 14 40 60, daily May-Sep (Oct-Apr, closed Sun). Mon-Sat Oct-Feb 0900-1230, 1330-1700; Feb-Jun, and Sep 0900-1300, 1400-1800; Jul-Aug 0900-1900. Sun 0930-1300, 1400-1730.*

Places in Dieppe → *For listings, see pages 47-49.*

Château-Musée
ⓘ *Rue de Chastes, T02 35 06 61 99. Jun-Sep 1000-1200 and 1400-1800, Oct-May Wed-Mon 1000-1200 and 1400-1700. €4, €2 concessions, under 12s free.*
Rising on a cliff at Dieppe's western edge, the flint-and-sandstone Château dominates the town. It has been so damaged, repaired, altered and expanded over the centuries that it's hard to imagine the original fortress built here in the 10th century by Richard the Fearless, Duke of Normandy. The oldest part is the 10th- to 12th-century west tower; the main structure is largely 15th century, though its northwest tower dates from the 14th century and the curtain walls were extended in the 17th century to incorporate the square 13th-century St-Rémy Tower. The structure survived bombardment by the British in 1694 and 1942, and is today the town's museum, divided into sections covering different themes.

The principal exhibition is of 16th- to 19th-century Dieppe ivories. The town was renowned for its skilled ivory carvers, whose clever, intricate work is still a delight to see: statues, model ships, boxes and miniature portraits, as well as a multitude of ornaments, tools and household objects. Several of the finer pieces are copies of well-known sculptures or popular images of their day, such as the lovely 18th-century Four Seasons.

Other sections deal with the maritime history of the town, and there are many good paintings, often on a Dieppe waterfront theme, by artists who frequented the town, including Renoir, Sisley, Sickert, Pissarro, Dufy, Courbet and many others, with a separate section devoted to lithographs by Georges Braque.

Oscar Wilde's Dieppe

It was to Dieppe that Oscar Wilde fled on being released from prison in 1897. Many old friends and acquaintances were here, including James McNeill Whistler, Walter Sickert and Aubrey Beardsley, and the art critic Robert Ross, to whom he handed the manuscript of *De Profundis*. He perhaps believed he would be welcomed, but it is said that most of the Dieppe community, including many former friends, shunned him, embarrassed by his imprisonment for homosexuality. His favourite haunts were the big and lively Café des Tribunaux that dominates place du Puits Salé, and quiet Café Suisse on the Arcade la Bourse quayside – both are still there. Wilde moved to Berneval-sur-Mer, 10 km away, then an isolated cliff-top village, to work on *The Ballad of Reading Gaol*.

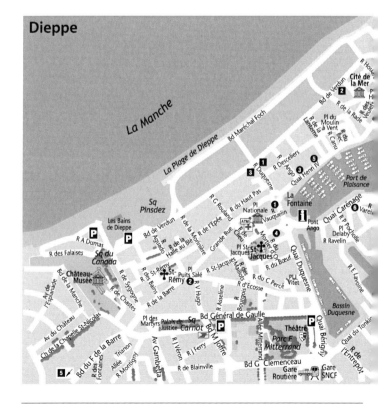

Dieppe

Dieppe raid: Operation Jubilee

On 19 August 1942, more than 5000 Canadian commandos and 1000 British launched a surprise attack on Dieppe and the neighbouring coast between Varengeville and Berneval. With considerable air and navy support, their objective was to breach and destroy German coastal defences, take prisoners, capture German planning documents and gather intelligence. Landing at 0500, they were defeated later the same morning without achieving any useful objectives. By the end of the day more than 1000 of the commandos were dead, over 600 wounded and some 2000 taken prisoner. Their air support lost 106 aircraft, while the Luftwaffe lost 48. Following the catastrophe, the one lesson learned was the strength of German defences on the Channel coast.

Cité de la Mer
① 37 rue de l'Asile Thomas, T02 35 06 93 20, estrancitedelamer.fr. Daily 1000-1200 and 1400-1800. €5.80, €4.50 concessions, €3.50 4-16.

Don't imagine a lavish sealife centre – despite the name, this modest rainy-day museum is scientific and technical, and mainly devoted to maritime rather than marine life. Most exhibits and displays deal with boat building and fishing, and explain all about tides and sea currents and their impact on the coast.

Right bank
The animated popular quaysides of Dieppe are on the port's west side – the left bank of the River Arques from which the harbour was carved. Cross the two bridges – Pont Ango and Pont Colbert – to the right bank to reach the little district of Le Pollet, a cluster of lanes of old redbrick and flint cottages that make up the fishermen's quarter. Climb up from here to one of the town's most distinctive landmarks, visible from far out at sea – the sailors' small cliff-top chapel, Notre-Dame de Bon Secours. This quiet, touching place of prayer, overlooking the harbour, is also a place of remembrance. It contains a memorial to every Dieppe seaman lost at sea since 1876, including whole trawlers missing with all their crew.

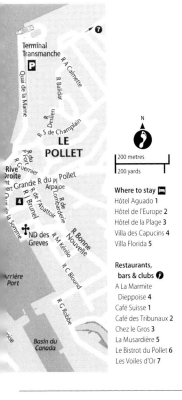

Terminal Transmanche 🅿

Quai de la Marne
R A Calmette
R Balidar
R S Desseaux
R-S de Champlain

LE POLLET

R du Cuernier
P du Prieuré
Rivel Droite
R Grande R du Pl Pollet
R de l'Abattoir
R de Lombarderie
R Brunel
R D. de la Somme
Arpajoe
R Bonne Nouvelle
R M Kéréio
✝ ND des Greves
R C Bloud
R C Robbe

Arrière Port

Basin du Canada

N

200 metres
200 yards

Where to stay ▭
Hôtel Aguado 1
Hôtel de l'Europe 2
Hôtel de la Plage 3
Villa des Capucins 4
Villa Florida 5

Restaurants, bars & clubs ❼
A La Marmite Dieppoise 4
Café Suisse 1
Café des Tribunaux 2
Chez le Gros 3
La Musardière 5
Le Bistrot du Pollet 6
Les Voiles d'Or 7

❼

Eglise St-Jacques

① 22 rue Boucherie, T02 32 14 63 00. Usually open during the day, free.

Dieppe's large parish church, between Grand'Rue and the fishing port, is a striking Flamboyant presence in the town. It has been much damaged and repaired over the centuries, yet remains an attractive example of the evolution of Gothic architecture from the 13th to 16th centuries, and serves as a monument to Dieppe's past prosperity. There's a good rose window over the central doorway. The interior is worn and damaged, but in use. Frescoes of the Stations of the Cross survive on pillars. The high nave of pale stone dates from the origins of the building, while the elaborate side chapels at the eastern end are the final touches. In one of the side chapels, a memorial honours those who died on the ill-fated Dieppe raid in 1942. Out of keeping with the rest is a remarkable Renaissance carved frieze, thought to have been rescued from Jehan Ango's own private palace when it was destroyed by British bombardment in 1694. The carvings show native people of Brazil and the Caribbean, probably encountered by Ango on his voyages.

Dieppe listings

For hotel and restaurant price codes and other relevant information, see pages 10-14.

🛏 Where to stay

Dieppe *p42, map p44*

€€ Hôtel Aguado, bd de Verdun, T02 35 84 27 00, hoteldieppe.com. Ideally situated just a moment's walk from the port, the town centre and the beach, this popular, inexpensive and rather dated 3-star straddles a side street. The main attraction is its position, not the amenities. It offers a choice of modest, homely rooms – perhaps a little too well-worn – either facing the beach or facing the town. Friendly and helpful reception.

€€ Hôtel de l'Europe, bd de Verdun, T02 32 90 19 19, hoteldieppe.com. The 2-star Europe has an unmissable wood-clad façade. Inside, decor is light and uncluttered, with a beach-resort feel. The spacious, sea-view rooms are smart and comfortably furnished.

€€-€ Hôtel de le Plage, bd de Verdun, T02 35 84 18 28, plagehotel.fr.st Modernized, attractive and pleasant, this affordable beachfront hotel makes a good base for Dieppe's town centre. Rooms are simple, brightly decorated, and adequately equipped. There's free Wi-Fi throughout.

Chambres d'hôtes

€€ Villa des Capucins, rue des Capucins, T02 35 82 16 52, villa-des-capucins.fr. This charming and attractive red-brick cottage in the evocative Le Pollet area is a cosy guesthouse, near to the heart of things yet away from the bustle of the town centre. It has a lovely garden.

€€ Villa Florida, Chemin du Golf, T02 35 84 40 37, lavillaflorida.com. Perfect for the golf course, this unusual B&B is a *chambre d'hôte de charme*. It has very comfortable, richly furnished rooms and the proprietor is a keen fan of yoga.

🍴 Restaurants

Dieppe *p42, map p44*

€€€ A La Marmite Dieppoise, rue St-Jean, T02 35 84 24 26. Tue-Sat Sun lunch and dinner, Sun lunch, closed 20 Jun-3 Jul, 21 Nov-9 Dec, 8-16 Feb. Tucked away in a little street between the church and the port, the restaurant gives its name to its very own culinary invention, a rich stew of lobster, mussels and several kinds of fish with crème fraîche sauce. Arguably, it's well worth coming to try it. The rest of the menu, though, is unremarkable, and prices are on the high side. The best of the desserts is a warm, home-made apple tart with a delicious cream. Tables rather close together. Sometimes indifferent service. Decor, relieved by romantic touches like candles, is faux historic, with bare brick, tile floors and beams.

€€€ Les Voiles d'Or, Chemin de la Falaise, T02 35 84 16 84, lesvoilesdor.fr. Wed-Sat lunch and dinner, Sun lunch, closed 2 weeks end Nov. High on the right bank, near the Notre Dame de Bon Secours chapel, this modern Michelin-starred restaurant is comfortable and stylish, with polished pale wood and hanging *voiles d'or* – golden sails. There are two well-prepared set menus, constantly changing as they reflect what's best in the market that day.

€€€-€€ Le Bistrot du Pollet, rue Tête de Boeuf, T02 35 84 68 57. Tue-Sat lunch and dinner, closed 2 weeks in Apr, 2 weeks in Aug, 10 days in Jan. On the island in the harbour, this convivial little bistro packed with diners is a top spot for eating out in Dieppe. Decor is on a seafaring theme. Cooking is good, with plenty of hearty traditional Normandy fare, *dieppoise* sauces, fresh fish and generous portions.

€€ Chez le Gros, quai Henri IV, T02 35 82 28 03. Lunch and dinner. Dieppe harbour is packed with modest fish and shellfish restaurants attracting tourists rather than locals. This waterfront wine bar and bistro

looks like a plain and simple café, but it's quite an exception – authentic French cooking that's as much about foie gras and *magret de canard* as the ubiquitous *moules-frites*.
€ La Musardière, quai Henri IV, T02 35 82 94 14, restaurant-la.com. Feb-Jun and Sep-Dec Wed-Sun lunch and dinner, daily Jul-Aug. Small, brightly lit, here's the classic cheap and cheerful fish and shellfish restaurant on the quayside, with friendly service and affordable set menus.

Cafés and bars
Café Suisse, arcades de la Bourse, T02 35 84 10 69. Subject of a painting by Walter Sickert in 1914, this one-time haunt of Oscar Wilde – when he wanted to get away from the smart set – survives as a classic, correct local brasserie, popular with locals. At mealtimes it serves simple traditional fare at modest prices. Outdoor tables are under an arcade.
Café des Tribunaux, du Puits Salé, T02 32 14 44 65. The tall, attractive, gabled tavern has been the haunt of many great names of art and literature. It's a smart, well-kept place, with a restored pre-war look inside, where stained-glass panels encircle an upper gallery. There are wrought-iron tables and chairs on the little square outside. It remains a lively, atmospheric, dominant presence in the town centre, with a view on to Grand'Rue. Excellent morning coffee, freshly squeezed orange juice and croissants. A painting of the *Café des Tribunaux* by Walter Sickert, showing the café as it was in 1890, hangs in the Tate Britain in London.

Entertainment

Dieppe *p42, map p44*
Casinos
Grand Casino Dieppe, 3 bd de Verdun, T02 32 14 48 00, casinodieppe.com. Mon-Thu 2100-0300, Fri 2100-0400, Sat 2000-0400, Sun 1600-0300. Near the sea at the foot of the château, Dieppe casino has slot machines and simple, modern gaming tables. It's far

from glamorous, but also has 2 restaurants, a piano bar and show theatre with occasional cabaret or entertainment.

Theatre and cinema
Dieppe Scène Nationale (DSN), quai Bérigny, T02 35 82 04 43, dsn.asso.fr. Tue-Sun 1400-1830. At the end of the harbour, this is the principal venue in Dieppe for arts events, stage shows, world music concerts, drama, modern dance and a full programme of arts performances and family entertainment. There's also a cinema showing a wide variety of new art and popular films as well as cinema classics. If you want to see English-language films, note that 'VO' means a film is shown in its original language.

Festivals

Dieppe *p42, map p44*
Kite festival, the tourist office for the latest festival information, or visit dieppe-cerf-volant.org. Filling the sky with scores of curious shapes and wild colours, Dieppe Kite Festival is held in **Sep** in even-numbered years, and attracts kite-flying experts from all over the world.

Shopping

Dieppe *p42, map p44*
Food and drink
Epicier Olivier, rue St-Jacques, T02 35 84 22 55, olivierdieppe.com. Tue-Sat 0800-1230 and 1400-1915, Sat no lunchtime closing, Mon afternoons in Jul-Aug. This respected *épicerie fine* with its traditional tiled façade specializes in the best of fine foods. Cheeses are a speciality, but you'll find here too butter sold off the block, fromage blanc and crème fraîche ladled from tubs, as well as coffees, teas, Calvados and local produce. Service is brisk but helpful.

Market

Dieppe's traditional Sat market attracts shoppers from across the region. Stalls run the length of Grand'Rue into place du Puits Salé, place Nationale, place St-Jacques, rue St-Jacques and the side streets. You'll find fresh produce from farms and fishing boats, fine displays of farm-made butter, charcuterie and cheeses (especially the local treat, Neufchâtel), baked goods, farm cider and apple juice, flowers, and stalls selling cooked dishes, especially hot roasted free-range chicken. Many of the fruit and vegetables are *bio* (organic). Other stalls offer honey and conserves, leather goods, kitchenware, CDs, souvenirs and clothes.

⏺ What to do

Dieppe *p42, map p44*
Fishing
Quayside firms run fishing trips and sea cruises. Ask at the tourist office for latest details.

Golf
Golf de Dieppe-Pourville, 51 route de Pourville, T02 35 84 25 05, golf-dieppe.com. Daily all year 0900-1800. This renowned high-quality 18-hole golf course was established in 1897. Considered a fairly challenging course, it hosts competitions Mar-Oct.

Petit Train tour
Petit Train Touristique de Dieppe, quai Henri-IV (beside tourist office), T02 35 04 56 08. Mid May-mid Oct, 1130-1730. €6, €4 child (3-10). All aboard for a fun ride around town. The tour lasts about 1 hr and takes in the beach and town centre sights.

Thermal baths
Les Bains des Docks, quai de la Réunion, T02 32 79 29 55, vert-marine.com/les-bains-des-docks-le-havre-76. Sep-Jun Mon and Wed 0900-2100, Tue, Thu and Fri 1200-2100, Sat-Sun 0900-1900; Jul-Aug daily 1000-2000. €5.30, €4.30 child 8-12 (under 8s free). Aqua-gym is open only for certain periods during the day Mon-Sat. This beautiful gleaming white dockside public baths was designed by a leading modern architect, Jean Nouvel. It has several indoor and outdoor pools of different temperatures, including a heated outdoor Olympic pool, as well as sports and play areas, an 'aqua-gym' for fitness sessions in the water and treatment rooms.

ⓘ Directory

Dieppe *p42, map p44*
Hospital Centre Hospitalier de Dieppe, av Pasteur, T02 32 14 76 76, ch-dieppe.fr.
Pharmacy The most centrally located pharmacy is La Grande Pharmacie, 15-17 place Nationale, T02 35 84 11 20. pharmacie-dieppe.com.

Côte d'Albâtre

Stretching along the whole length of the Seine Maritime seafront, this coast is called the Côte d'Albâtre (Alabaster Coast) simply because alabaster is so white. The chalky plateau of the Pays de Caux reaches the English Channel in an abrupt, majestic line of soaring white cliffs. Sometimes they jut into the sea, sometimes they are set back behind coves and beaches, and sometimes, where there are deep cuts and breaks in the chalk, fishing ports have prospered. The harbours at the foot of the cliffs were established long ago – Fécamp, for example, has been a busy port since Roman times. Several beach resorts also sprang up along the Côte d'Albâtre more than a century ago and have remained popular, such as Etretat, best known for the way the waves have eaten its chalky rock into curious shapes. On the top of the white cliffs, lush vegetation grows and quiet little villages watch out over the sea. Over the centuries, most have made their living from both farming and fishing, although many also have a long tradition of well-to-do outsiders building fine villas and mansions as tranquil hideaways. Among the grandest of all is the lavish home of 16th-century privateer Jehan Ango at Varengeville.

Jehan Ango

A shipbuilder's son and, at first, a shipbuilder himself, Jehan (or Jean) Ango was born in Dieppe in 1480. He became one of the many great seafaring traders and adventurers of the town, making frequent expeditions to Africa and the Americas. This represented a challenge to the Portuguese, who maintained that they alone had the right to trade off the African coast. Ango built a vast fortune, initially through the piracy of captains he equipped and sponsored, notably Jean Fleury, who seized Aztec treasures being taken from Mexico to Spain.

François I, the French king, wishing to respond to the Portuguese dominance in Atlantic trade, authorized Ango to seize all Portuguese trading vessels

he encountered in the Atlantic. Jehan Ango's huge fleet of up to 100 vessels proceeded to terrorize Atlantic shipping, seizing 300 Portuguese trading vessels and their cargo. Ships of other nations, including England and Holland, were also seized. Jehan Ango's fortune increased to royal levels, and the king appointed him Governor of Dieppe. He built two homes, one in Dieppe and one (which survives) in Varengeville. His eminent house guests included François I himself, who made Ango a Viscount. However, the king also felt himself entitled to call on Ango's fortune, and pressed him for such large loans that by the end of his life Ango had little left. He died in 1551 and was buried in Dieppe's Eglise St-Jacques.

Varengeville-sur-Mer → For listings, see pages 54-56.

A pretty wooded cliff-top area of hidden cottages, gardens, footpaths and villas, Varengeville is a delight. Arriving from nearby Dieppe, 8 km east, a sign points from the road into a lane between an avenue of trees, leading to the Manoir d'Ango, the grand home of the privateer Jehan Ango, who grew rich by seizing hundreds of Portuguese, English and other merchant vessels (see box, above). Although arranged in the form of a traditional Normandy fortified farm enclosure, the building is in 16th-century Italian Renaissance style, with raised arched galleries forming a loggia on one side, and plenty of fine decoration. In black and white stone, it's arranged around an impressive courtyard at the centre of which is a huge dovecote. Only the grounds may be visited (March to November).

Another lane leads through the trees to the **Parc des Moutiers** ① *T02 35 85 10 02, boisdesmoutiers.com, mid-Mar to mid-Nov, 1000-2000, but ticket office open 1000-1200, 1400-1800, €10, children (7-15) €4*, 9 ha of cleverly laid out botanic gardens, with rare trees, flowering bushes and sea views. The park is mostly the work of English landscape gardener Gertrude Jekyll (1843-1932). There's always something in bloom, from March to November. Paths wind among colourful flowering bushes and extraordinary 6-m-high rhododendrons. An unusual mansion at the centre of the park, with curious corner windows and many English country house touches, was built in 1898 by the great Imperial architect Sir Edwin Lutyens.

Perhaps the loveliest sight in Varengeville is the lonely little parish church, Eglise de St-Valéry, perched on the edge of a high cliff rising from the seashore. There's a magnificent view of the coast from here. Inside the simple church it's immediately obvious that the building dates from two very different periods, as two naves and two choirs have been stuck together, one 11th-century Romanesque, of pale stone, and one 13th- to 15th-century Gothic, partly in brick. Round arches with strangely carved columns separate the two sections. In the south choir aisle is a beautiful modern stained-glass window depicting *The Tree of Jesse*, by the leading Cubist artist Georges Braque, who lived in Varengeville.

The church is surrounded by its simple cemetery, in which Braque (1883-1963) is buried beside his wife. Nearby are several other interesting graves, including that of the composer Albert Roussel (1869-1937).

St-Valéry-en-Caux → *For listings, see pages 54-56.*

After being destroyed during the British retreat to Dunkirk, St-Valéry, 34 km south of Dieppe on D925, was rebuilt and is today a thriving fishing port and marina, overlooked by large modern hotel. The town's new church, built in 1963, has a striking wall of stained glass. There's a **tourist information office** ① *quai d'Amont, T02 35 97 00 63, plateaudecauxmaritime.com.*

The coast and countryside nearby are impressive and beautiful. On the beach, magnificent white cliffs rise up, while climbing from the shore in places are pretty villages and lanes, for example at Veules-les-Roses. At the roadside in Veules a memorial commemorates 38 Commonwealth soldiers who died in 1940 during the Dieppe raid.

Fécamp → *For listings, see pages 54-56.*

Although a busy, industrial fishing port, Fécamp, 30 km north of Le Havre on D940, is also an old resort town, enclosed by white cliffs. It provides the background to several novels by Guy de Maupassant, who was born here. The harbour is the town's focal point, and here a good deal of France's daily catch of fresh cod is landed. The town rises steeply from the waterfront. There's a good market in the town centre on Saturdays, centred on place Bellet. There is a **tourist information office** ① *quai Sadi Carnot, T02 35 28 51 01, fecamptourisme.com.*

Eglise Abbatiale de la Trinité
① *Place des Ducs Richard, T02 35 28 84 39. Approx Apr-Sep 0900-1900, Oct-Mar 0900-1200 and 1400-1700.*

Fécamp was put on the map in the early seventh century when pilgrims flocked to see a lead casket, supposedly containing 'drops of the Holy Blood', which had been washed ashore in the hollowed-out trunk of what was said to be a fig tree. A monastery was built to protect the Precious Blood, as it became known. In the 11th century, Richard II of England built the Eglise de la Trinité to house the relic. He also re-founded the monastery as a huge abbey, the first under Benedictine rule. It grew immensely wealthy as vast numbers of pilgrims came to revere the Precious Blood.

The abbey church was later reconstructed in Flamboyant Gothic style, and has been much altered over the centuries, but still contains some lovely vestiges of the original. It is a huge building, its white stone interior tall and soaring in design and, at 127 m, one of the longest churches in Europe. Here you'll find the tombs of both Duke Richard I and Duke Richard II, as well as some superb stone carving and notable artworks, especially the richly detailed 15th-century *Dormition of the Virgin*. Along the length are many side chapels. Even today, pilgrims come here to see the Precious Blood, in the small, carved white marble *Tabernacle du Précieux Sang.*

Palais Bénédictine

ⓘ *110 rue Alexandre le Grand, T02 35 10 26 10, benedictine.fr. Daily 1030-1245 and 1400-1800, slightly longer hours in summer, shorter in winter (closed 1 Jan-10 Feb), €7.20, €3.20 child, under 12s free.*

In the 16th century, Fécamp's Benedictine community used local wild plants to create their very own liqueur, and called it, quite simply, Bénédictine. The abbey's distillery soon became, and still is, a thriving business, since 1863 unconnected to the monks. Today the distilling takes place in a wildly ornate 19th-century mock-Gothic palace called the Palais Bénédictine, which also houses an eclectic museum on the history of the Benedictines and their liqueur. In the museum, astonishing displays include precious ivories, a 15th-century illuminated Book of Hours, and several painted panels of the same period, finely worked silver and gold, priceless alabaster pieces, ancient manuscripts, a collection of paintings dating back to the 14th century, and a gallery of modern art. Afterwards, pop into the airy tasting room to the right of the entrance for a tot of rich, sweet, acerbic Benedictine (free with your entry ticket, or €2 without).

Etretat → *For listings, see pages 54-56.*

The great feature of this long-established small resort, 29 km north of Le Havre on D940, which is popular with weekenders all year round, is its green-topped white cliffs, carved into curious shapes by long millennia of wind and waves. Most striking, cut out of the chalk of the Falaise d'Aval at the south end of the beach, is a tall offshore needle of white rock called the Aiguille; and the Porte d'Aval, a natural archway that looks like an elephant's trunk sticking into the water. At the north end, the charming little 11th- and 12th-century Notre-Dame de la Garde chapel stands alone on top of the spectacular Falaise d'Amont cliff, which looks like a small open doorway in a huge white wall in the sea. Clearly marked (but steep) cliff footpaths allow you to fully appreciate the beauty and grandeur of the setting. A pleasant promenade behind the beach runs part of the way between the two cliffs. South of town, the Manneport, another curious archway in the sea, can be reached on a cliff-top path, which is a section of long-distance footpath GR21.

In the late 19th and early 20th century, Etretat was one of those thoroughly elegant little Normandy seaside resorts patronized by the most distinguished people, its breezy marine freshness adding to its appeal. While those days are long gone, the town remains bright and busy, and preserves a refined air. There's a golf course and a casino. In town, place du Marché is wonderfully picturesque, with a wooden former covered market. There is a **tourist information office** ⓘ *place Maurice Guillard, T02 35 27 05 21, etretat.net.*

Well-known artists and writers also came frequently to Etretat in its heyday. Guy de Maupassant, who spent his teenage years here, later took his family for summer holidays at Etretat. Victor Hugo and Gustave Flaubert both declared how much they loved the Etretat seaside, and stream of Impressionists came here to paint, among them Monet, Courbet, Delacroix and Degas.

Côte d'Albâtre listings

For hotel and restaurant price codes and other relevant information, see pages 10-14.

⬤ Where to stay

Varengeville-sur-Mer *p51*

€ La Terrasse, de Vasterival, T02 35 85 12 54, hotel-restaurant-la-terrasse.com. Quiet, comfortable, friendly accommodation tucked away in countryside on the cliff top at the western edge of Varengeville, this country-house style hotel has fine views of the sea. Decor is simple and modern. There's a very attractive restaurant with good cooking, see below.

Fécamp *p52*

€€€ Grand Pavois, quai Vicomte, T02 35 10 01 01, hotel-grand-pavois.com. A smart 3-star hotel overlooking the harbour, the Grand Pavois has generously sized rooms with plain and simple modern furnishings and decor. Some have a particularly fine view. There's a relaxing piano bar on the ground floor.

€€-€ Mer, bd Albert 1er, T02 35 28 24 64, hotel-dela-mer.com. This unpretentious modern 2-star is right on the beachfront, with the children's play area next door, and right above a busy brasserie. The casino is not far away. Rooms are simply but pleasantly decorated and adequately equipped, some with sea views and balcony, though the rear rooms have a less pleasant prospect. There's free Wi-Fi.

€€ Hôtel Normandy, 4 av Gambetta, T02 35 29 55 11, normandy-fecamp.com. Simple and unpretentious modern comfort is on offer for very modest prices in this white-fronted former coaching inn standing beside the church of St-Etienne, on a corner near the port. Some rooms have sea views. Downstairs is the restaurant and brasserie Le Maupassant, see page 55.

Etretat *p53*

€€€ Domaine St-Clair – Le Donjon, Chemin de St-Clair, T02 35 27 08 23, ledonjon-etretat.fr. Luckily donjon means not 'dungeon', but 'keep', rather a grandiose name for this splendid Anglo-Norman country house and belle epoque holiday villa with views across the town to the sea. Rooms are comfortably equipped and very varied; most are large – vast would be a better description in some cases. The hotel stands in its own attractive grounds, and has a heated pool, a library and an elegant gourmet restaurant. There is golf and riding nearby.

€€€-€€ Dormy House, du Havre, T02 35 27 07 88, etretat-hotel.com. A cliff-edge position with wonderful views adds to the appeal of this handsome 19th-century manor house in its own grounds. Rooms are spacious and comfortable, varying from relatively simple to luxurious, so there's a big price range. Standard rooms look out on the grounds, while superior rooms have a sea view. The hotel has an excellent restaurant, see page 55.

€€-€ Manoir de la Salamandre/ La Résidence, bd Coty, T02 35 27 02 87, hotelresidenceetretat.com.This picturesque half-timbered manor house preserves numerous historic touches, exposed beams, polished wood and 4-poster beds. Rooms are charming and adequately equipped, very varied in size, some presented as family rooms. The ground floor is Restaurant la Salamandre.

⓪ Restaurants

Varengeville-sur-Mer *p51*

€€ La Terrasse, de Vasterival, T02 35 85 12 54, hotel-restaurant-la-terrasse.com. Daily lunch and dinner. In the Hôtel la Terrasse (see above), this attractive, spacious restaurant, hung with pale fabrics, has lovely views out to sea. The accomplished and skilful menus focus on fresh local fish and shellfish, with dishes like mussels in roquefort sauce, local specialities such as *sole à la dieppoise*, and favourite desserts such as tarte tatin.

Fécamp *p52*
€€ Auberge de la Rouge, route du Havre (corner of rue Bois de Boclon), 2 km from Fécamp, T02 35 28 07 59, auberge-rouge.fr. Tue-Sat 1215-1330 and 1915-2100, Sun 1915-2100. In the pretty, rustic setting of a flower-decked old coaching inn there are plenty of wooden beams and exposed brick. Here good traditional French cooking is served in three cosy dining rooms, using all the best ingredients of the market.
€€-€ Le Maupassant, av Gambetta, T02 35 29 55 11, normandy-fecamp.com. Mon-Sat all day. On the ground floor of the Hôtel Normandy (see page 54), this popular restaurant and brasserie serves classic French and Normandy fare, such as *foie gras* followed by cod in cream sauce, with some well-priced set menus.
€€-€ Le Vicomte, rue Président R Coty, T02 35 28 47 63. Mon-Tue, Thu-Sat for lunch and dinner, closed end Apr and beginning May, 2 weeks in Aug, Christmas and New Year. Tasty, classic French bistro cooking is served at this busy, appealing little place not far from the port area. What you'll be offered all depends on what's best in the market – menus of the day are written on a blackboard.

Etretat *p53*
€€€ Dormy House, du Havre, T02 35 27 07 88, etretat-hotel.com. Lunch and dinner. The restaurant in this cliff-edge hotel on the south side of town has magnificent sea views, and a choice of tempting set menus. Dishes are delicate and imaginative, with plenty of fresh fish and local touches, such as fresh cod open ravioli with mushrooms and leeks cooked with cider and shellfish sauce. Desserts include roast apricots with lavender ice cream.

€€ Le Bicorne, 5 bd Président R Coty, T02 35 29 62 22, hws.fr/lebicorne. Thu-Mon for lunch and dinner (daily in school holidays). In a warm and cosy setting of polished timber and wood panels, excellent fish and seafood dishes – and plenty of classic meat dishes as well – are presented in striking, colourful arrangements. Try the monkfish with pommeau sauce. Service is warm and genuine.
€€-€ La Salamandre, bd Coty, T02 35 27 17 07, lasalamandreetretat.com. Lunch and dinner. In a picturesque half-timbered manor house in the town centre, the restaurant of this small hotel has rustic, cosy decor of exposed beams, polished wood and gingham cloths. Everything served is certified organic, or is the fresh catch of the day. Dishes have a simple, natural quality, such as three fresh fish grilled with olive oil, and there's a vegetarian selection.

⊙ Entertainment

Etretat *p53*
Casinos
JOA Casino, 1 rue Adolphe Boissaye, T02 35 27 00 54, joa-casino.com/Casinos-Loisirs/ CASINO-JOA-D-ETRETAT. Daily 1000-0100 (0300 Fri, Sat and eve of national holidays). With a pub-like feel, Etretat's casino has slot machines, some simple gaming tables, a bar and restaurant, as well as a programme of evening entertainment like a disco or jazz. The best feature is its position on the beach, with views towards the arch cliffs.

⊙ Shopping

Fécamp *p52*
Food and drink
Benedictine Distillery (Palais Bénédictine), 110 rue Alexandre le Grand, T02 35 10 26 10, benedictine.fr. Early Feb to Mar and mid-Oct to 31 Dec 1030-1145, 1400-1700; Apr to early Jul and end Aug to mid-Oct 1000-1200, 1400-1730; early Jul to end Aug 1000-1800. Closed Jan-early Feb.

The Benedictine distillery has its own boutique selling bottles of the liqueur, and a selection of unusual treats and delicacies filled or flavoured with it, such as 12 chocolates filled with Benedictine.

⚙ What to do

Fécamp *p52*
Boat tours
Ask at the tourist office for their choice of 2-hr mini-cruises giving views of the coast and port.

Etretat *p53*
Golf
Golf d'Etretat, route du Havre, T02 35 27 04 89, golfetretat.com. Apr-Aug 0830-1900 daily (except as affected by special events and competitions), Sep-Oct Wed-Mon 0900-1800, Nov-Mar Wed-Mon 0900-1700. On top of high chalk cliffs beside Etretat, with their dramatic arches stepping into the waves, is spread the green expanse of the town's golf course. Founded in 1908, it soon became prestigious: many of its members were British aristocrats. It is still highly rated, in a remarkable setting, and the clubhouse has an excellent restaurant.

❶ Directory

Fécamp *p52*
Hospital Centre Hospitalier Intercommunal du Pays des Hautes Falaises, 100 ave du Président Mitterrand, T02 35 10 90 00, ch-fecamp.fr.
Pharmacy Pharmacie de la Marine, 65 quai Bérigny, T02 35 28 00 68.

Le Havre

Le Havre 100 years ago was a bustling, picturesque sea port and the home of the first Impressionists – some of their views of it can be seen in the important Musée Malraux. Today, thanks to its vast industrial areas, travellers often take the view that Le Havre is a place to get away from rather than go to. Nor is it Le Havre's fault that the 16th-century town was almost completely destroyed by Allied bombing in September 1944 (killing more than 4000 residents in one week) and had to be quickly and cheaply rebuilt. However, the rebuilding was entrusted to Auguste Perret, a 70-year-old follower of the architect Le Corbusier who shared his passion for reinforced concrete. Perret's vision resulted in a Quartier Moderne at the heart of the city laid out as an evenly spaced grid of long straight streets lined with not unattractive but monotonously similar buildings, often the same height along any given street – nearly all five, six or seven storeys high, with a profusion of balconies. There is occasional relief in the form of broad avenues, squares and parks. Le Havre also has a pleasant sand and pebble beach backed by gardens, and a charming, bustling waterfront, close to the main street, avenue Foch. Whether Auguste Perret's Le Havre is a success remains controversial. Nevertheless, in 2005 it was named a World Heritage Site.

Arriving in La Havre

Getting there
The **Gare Routière** is at boulevard de Strasbourg, T02 35 26 67 23, and the **train station** at Cours Lafayette/Cours République, T02 35 22 35 00.

Getting around
Within the greater urban area of Le Havre, an extensive public transport network of buses (including six all-night routes) and two modern tramlines from early in the morning until late in the evening is operated, by **LiA** (**Les Lignes de l'Agglo**) ① *T02-35 22 35 00, transports-lia.fr.*

Tourist information
There's a **tourist information office** ① *186 bd Clémenceau, T02 32 74 04 04, lehavretourisme. com, Mon-Sat 0900-1900, Sun 1000-1230 and 1430-1800, Nov-Easter closes 1830 weekdays, mornings only on Sun.*

Places in Le Havre → *For listings, see pages 60-62.*

Musée des Beaux Arts – André Malraux
① *2 bd Clemenceau, T02 35 19 62 62, muma-lehavre.fr/blog-50ans, Wed-Mon 1100-1800 (1900 Sat-Sun), closed national holidays, €5, €3 concessions, under 26s free.*
Built overlooking the waterside at the very mouth of the Seine, the glass and steel museum – with a large concrete sculpture in front – offers a cool, light-filled space to display a superb collection of Impressionist and Post-Impressionist artworks from some of its greatest names. Other areas are devoted to painting and sculpture from the 16th-20th centuries and contemporary art. The different galleries are linked by walkways like those on a ship. In particular there are over 200 works by Eugène Boudin, as well as several good examples of Monet, Renoir and Pissarro, and other Impressionists. Among Post-Impressionists, another Le Havre native, the Fauvist Raoul Dufy, is very well represented, with numerous paintings and drawings, many inspired by local life. Other Fauvists on display include Van Dongen and Friesz.

Eglise St-Joseph
① *Bd François 1er, T02 32 74 04 05, daily 1000-1800 (except during special ceremonies).*
The city's most visible landmark, its distinctive octagonal spire rising to 110 m, has been acclaimed one of Europe's greatest monuments to the post-war reconstruction. This large church, built of concrete and completed in 1957 after Perret's death, is arguably his masterpiece, although whether it can be called beautiful remains debatable. Outwardly the shape resembles a rocket, while the spacious interior seems more like an auditorium than a church. Perret dedicated it to the memory of the victims of the 1944 bombings. He pictured the tall slender spire as a lighthouse – 6500 shards of coloured glass set into the concrete supposedly allowing ever-changing light through the building. This works well on a bright sunny day, which causes a mosaic of colour to be scattered around the angular interior.

Appartement Témoin (the Show Flat)
① *186 bd Clemenceau, T02 35 22 31 22. Tours €3, on Wed, Sat and Sun 1400-1700 (tour starts every hr from 1 place de l'Hôtel de Ville) – book at tourist office.*

A rare and fascinating exhibit, Perret's Show Flat reveals the humane ambition that lay behind the architect's designs for the new Le Havre. Many of the revolutionary ideas he incorporated into his apartment blocks have now become normal: plenty of light, built-in kitchens, central heating, and chutes in which to throw rubbish. The flat is furnished with the inexpensive but stylish mass-produced furniture of the early 1950s, and all the latest mod cons of the period.

Ste-Adresse

Spread across the sea cliffs north of the city centre, this lofty, airy residential suburb has good views over the port and out to sea. Here the 19th-century Fort de Ste-Adresse – one of several forts built to defend the Seine estuary – has been laid out as an attractive park and botanic gardens called Les Jardins Suspendus (Hanging Gardens). Ideal for a rest or stroll, it features a wide variety of rare and exotic plants from around the world.

Le Havre listings

For hotel and restaurant price codes and other relevant information, see pages 10-14.

😴 Where to stay

Le Havre *p57*

€€€ Vent d'Ouest, rue de Caligny, T02 35 42 50 69, ventdouest.fr. In a typical *Quartier Moderne* building well placed near the main shopping area in avenue Foch and close to the waterfront, this quiet, friendly hotel has a bright marine feel. Rooms are sometimes on the small side, but are comfortably furnished in pine, in an attractive, homely style, especially those equipped with kitchenettes and intended for long stays. The hotel has a useful restaurant and bar.

€€€-€€ Pasino, Jules Ferry, T02 35 26 00 00, casinolehavre.com. Arty, chic and stylish, this comfortable, well-equipped modern hotel is part of the **Casino Partouche**, and has an atmosphere of self-indulgence and pleasure. Rooms are spacious, staff helpful, and there's free Wi-Fi. In addition to its casino, the hotel has 3 restaurants and a luxurious spa (closed Tue and Wed), where you can go straight from your room in a bathrobe.

€€ Art Hôtel (Best Western), rue Louis Brindeau, T02 35 22 69 44, art-hotel.fr. Quirky touches – for example, the elevator made to look like a shower cubicle – enliven the simple, decor at this *Quartier Moderne* building nearly opposite the entertainment complex Le Volcan. Furnishings are modern, some rooms small, and staff helpful.

€€ Novotel Le Havre Bassin Vauban, cours Lafayette, T02 35 19 23 23, novotel. com. With its blue neon sign illuminating the port near the station, the **Novotel** offers the modern comforts typical of this mid-range, well-priced chain. Interiors are designed to reflect Le Havre's 1950s modernity, and the restaurant aims for a modern style of cuisine.

€€ Terminus, cours de la République, T02 35 25 42 48, grand-hotel-terminus.fr. Ideal for a short stopover, this hotel opposite the railway station is functional and straightforward. It's popular with business travellers, with its reasonable prices, calm atmosphere and soothing, low-key decor. It has its own simple inexpensive restaurant and bar.

€ Richelieu, rue de Paris, T02 35 42 38 71, hotel-lerichelieu-76.com. Looking a little out of place in an arcaded row of shops, this little hotel offers small, basic but homely and comfortable rooms, brightly and individually decorated with tiny bathrooms attached. It has a friendly, genuine feel, is clean and well kept, provides free Wi-Fi and is located in the Quartier Moderne city centre.

🍴 Restaurants

Le Havre *p57*

€€€ Jean-Luc Tartarin, av Foch, T02 35 45 46 20, jeanluc-tartarin.com. Tue-Sat for lunch and dinner. Ambitious gastronomic cuisine has won this acclaimed restaurant a Michelin star. Shellfish is strongly featured. Speciality lobster and young pigeon dishes have striking exotic flavour combinations such as tea, coffee or cocoa. The slick, contemporary decor is in muted pale and dark chocolate tones.

€€€ La Petite Auberge, rue de Ste-Adresse, T02 35 46 27 32, lapetiteauberge-lehavre.fr. Tue-Sun 0900-2300, except Sun dinner and Wed lunch. Closed 3 weeks in summer, 1 week in autumn, 2 weeks in Feb. Towards the heights of Ste-Adresse, this cosy dining room of an old inn has a façade of painted wooden beams, plush decor and furnishing with rich cream and maroon colours and white napery. Fresh market produce is used to make a range of dishes such as rissoles of parma ham and ricotta.

€€ **Brasserie Pasino**, Jules Ferry, T02 35
26 00 00, casinolehavre.com. Daily 1200-
2400. This brasserie with harbour views
is one of 3 eating places in the **Casino
Hotel Partouche**. Affordable menus range
from brasserie classics and mixed grills to
Normandy specialities.

€ **L'Acrobate**, 77 rue Louis Brindeau,
T02 35 41 24 42. Mon-Sat 0900-2300.
This simple and unassuming city centre
brasserie attracts locals for a drink or a bite
to eat, and serves good simple French classic
dishes on a very reasonably priced set menu.

Cafés and bars

Beer and Billiards, rue René Coty, T02 35
42 44 88. Outside the Quartier Moderne,
this pub-like snooker bar is on 2 floors,
with a good selection of drinks, 17 billiard
tables, and major football matches shown
on big TV screens.

Le Chillou, rue Chillou, T02 35 41 75 49.
This small, long-established city centre bar
can become lively with locals popping in
for a drink or a snack. One of its attractions
is the patron's warm personality. Another is
the daily menu of home-cooked favourites
at modest prices.

🎵 Bars and clubs

Le Havre *p57*

A fast-changing dance club scene provides
late-night entertainment all week. Most
clubs are in the docks area, by the Bassin
du Commerce.

Wab Bar and Lobby Lounge, 33 rue d'Iéna,
T02 35 53 03 91, wablobbylounge.com.
Bar: Mon-Sat 1800-0200; **Lobby Lounge**:
Thu-Sat 2200-0500. This rather glamorous
clubby cocktail bar near the docks is the
place to relax with a drink or a meal and
enjoy a lounge ambience with an eclectic
mix of music from jazz to rock.

🎭 Entertainment

Le Havre *p57*
Music

Le Volcan – Le Havre National Stage,
Oscar Niemeyer, rue de Paris, T02 35 19
10 10, levolcan.com.Brilliant arts complex
inside 2 volcano-shaped structures,
the work of architect Oscar Niemeyer
(1907-2012; like Auguste Perret, he was
fascinated by the possibilities of concrete).
They stage performances of modern dance
and classical music. From 2011 to 2013,
performances were moved to the former
Le Havre ferry terminal (known for the
duration as **Le Volcan Maritime**) to allow
an extensive renovation of the Volcan
buildings. **Le Volcan Maritime** is at ave.
Lucien Corbeaux, T02 35 19 10 20.

🛍 Shopping

Le Havre *p57*

St-Vincent area between St-Roch public
park and the beach is packed with classy
little shops selling haute couture, gourmet
specialities, jewellery, art and antiques.

Market

The big, bustling street market in avenue
Réné Coty is held every Mon, Wed and Fri.

Shopping centres

Centre Commercial Grand Cap, du Bois au
Coq, T02 35 54 71 71, grandcap.fr. Mon-Sat
0930-1930, except Auchan: Mon-Sat 0830-
2130. For shopping under 1 roof, head to
the Grand Cap mall on the northern edge
of the city. There's an Auchan hypermarket,
and much else besides.

Espace Coty, René Coty, T02 32 74 86 87,
espacecoty-lehavre.com. Mon-Sat most
shops open 0930-2000. The area around
avenue Foch, rue de Paris and avenue
René Coty is full of chic fashion, accessories
and jewellery stores, as well as top-quality
gourmet food specialists, including a branch
of **Chocolatier Auzou**. Coty shopping

mall has 80 shops on 3 floors, as well as restaurants and cafés, plus a post office and a supermarket.

🕙 What to do

Le Havre *p57*
Cultural tours
Le Havre Ville d'art et d'histoire, 186 bd Clemenceau, T02 35 21 27 33, ville-lehavre.fr. Prices may vary slightly depending on the tour. Approx €5, €3 students, €3 child 12-18, under 12s €3 during summer school holidays, under 12s free at all other times, unemployed free. Visit to the Appartement Témoin €3, free for under 26s. Le Havre city council and tourist office run a full programme of guided visits to Le Havre's cultural and architectural attractions. Each tour lasts 1-1½ hrs and focuses on a single site or aspect of the city. There are also tours to the Hanging Gardens and Le Volcan arts centre. The tourist office can provide information and make bookings.

Petit Train tour
Office de Tourisme, 186 bd Clemenceau, T02 32 74 04 04, le-havre-tourism.com. Runs during school holidays only, usually needs to be booked in advance, €5.50, free under 13 years. The 'little train' snakes through the city to the sights on a choice of itineraries: for example, Le Havre World Heritage Site (1 hr), or Le Havre Ste-Adresse (45 mins).

ℹ Directory

Le Havre *p57*
Hospital (for general emergencies) Hôpital J Monod, 29 ave Pierre Mendés-France, Montvilliers, T02 32 73 32 32, ch-havre.fr. **Pharmacy** There are several pharmacies in the town centre, including in the main square, at 26 place de l'Hôtel de Ville (T02 35 42 46 78, pharmacie-havre.fr).

Lyons and Bray

On its east side, the wide open fields and occasional copses of Seine Maritime's high chalk plateaux give way to larger, denser wooded areas and more small-scale, varied cultivation. The extensive forests of Eu, Eawy and Lyons are among the most beautiful beech woods in France, cut across with footpaths and bridleways. The Pays de Bray, in Normandy's northeast corner, is a pretty, tranquil region of green fields, orchards, and meadows where cattle are reared for their rich milk, made into the gourmet cheese of Neufchâtel. From Neufchâtel to Gournay a striking depression is carved into the landscape, edged with a chalky ridge, known as the Boutonnière de Bray (the Bray Buttonhole). Among the few towns of any size in this area, Forges-les-Eaux has long been, as its name suggests, both an iron-working centre and a health-giving spa. The Pays de Bray merges and overlaps with the Pays de Lyons (which lies mainly in the Eure *département*), most of which is within the Forêt de Lyons, a 10,700-ha patchwork of ancient beech woods and bright cornfields. Within the forest, you'll find Mortemer Abbey, founded by a king and haunted by a ghostly queen, and the pretty little woodland town of Lyons-la-Forêt.

Green Avenue: London–Paris cycleway

A 408-km cycle path now runs all the way between Westminster Bridge in London and Notre Dame Cathedral in Paris. Designated as the Avenue Verte (sometimes locally known as La Route Verte), it takes a ferry from Newhaven to Dieppe and crosses Upper Normandy via the Pays de Bray. In France, the route mainly follows the route of a former railway line beside the D1 from Dieppe to Neufchâtel, continuing to Forges-les-Eaux, then towards Pontoise and Paris.

Abbaye de Mortemer (Mortemer Abbey)

① *T02 32 49 54 34, mortemer.free.fr. Exterior open 1330-1800, €6, €4 child 6-16 years; interior open on guided tours 1400-1800, May-Sep daily, Oct-Apr weekends only, additional €3.*

The Mortemer Cistercian community was founded in 1134 on grounds given for the purpose by Henry I. The monks, charged with maintaining the Forêt de Lyons as a hunting ground for the Dukes of Normandy, were responsible for much of its present-day appearance. They cleared land for cultivation, built hamlets and laid many tracks through the woodland. At the time of the Revolution, the abbey was largely destroyed and its stonework carted away for reuse.

The ruins of Mortemer are hidden in the woods just off the road to Les Andelys. Head southwards out of Lyons-la-Forêt on D2. The third turning on the left leads to a narrow lane which runs very steeply down to the valley of the Fouillebroc stream and a shallow lake created from the waters of the stream. Beside it stand fragments of imposing stone walls and arches, what remains of the original monastery where Henry I had the fateful dinner of lampreys (similar to eels), which killed him – he died in Lyons-la-Forêt. Attractive cloisters survive from the original building.

At a discreet distance stand late 17th-century buildings erected in an effort to re-establish the community. These today contain an interesting museum of monastic life, with deer and ponies wandering at liberty in the extensive grounds. The old monastery and its grounds are said to be haunted by a number ghosts of monks and even of a cat; the most distinguished ghostly presence is that of Queen (or Empress) Matilda of England, granddaughter of William the Conqueror, daughter of Henry I, mother of Henry II.

Château de Fleury-la-Forêt

① *About 7 km from Lyons-la-Forêt on D14, T02 32 49 63 91, chateau-fleury-la-foret.com. Open 1400-1800 (Jul-Aug daily, other months Sun only), closed mid-Nov to mid-Mar, €7, €6 child.*

A well-preserved 17th-century grand country house in elegant grounds, the building has kept its old wine cellars, chapel, kitchen and laundry, and today is the setting for a good museum of historic toys and dolls. In the château, three atmospheric, grandly furnished rooms are let as unusual and modestly priced chambres d'hôtes.

Château de Vascœuil – Centre d'Art et d'Histoire

① *Vascœuil, T02 35 23 62 35, chateauvascoeuil.com. Apr-Jul and Sep-Nov Wed-Sun 1430-1800, Jul-Aug daily 1000-1830. €8, €5.50 child/concessions, €20 family ticket.*

This charmingly restored, fortified stone-built 15th-century manor in Normandy style, standing in its handsome green park, has been an important contemporary art museum and cultural centre since 1970. In the grounds there's a large 17th-century circular dovecote as well as a sculpture park with some 50 works, including some by leading names of post-war art, among them Dali, Vasarely, Braque and Cocteau. The interior of the building is used from mid-March to mid-November for three annual contemporary art exhibitions – Spring, Summer and Autumn. Note that the name, Vascœuil, is pronounced with a silent 's'.

Close by is the attractive, busy village of Ry, which it is thought served as the model for Yonville l'Abbaye in Flaubert's Madame Bovary.

Forges-les-Eaux

Poised above the Bray 'buttonhole', Forges is in a lovely part of the Bray countryside. It gets the Forges of its name from the days when this was a centre of ironwork, but that ceased centuries ago. Today it's *les eaux*, the waters, which dominate at this modest country town, with a little spa resort complex on the south side. Run by casino operators Partouche, it includes a comfortable and well-equipped hotel with a wide range of spa treatments, as well as a casino and a good restaurant, all in a quiet and attractive setting at the edge of a park. There's a **tourist information office** ① *Rue Albert Bochet, T02 35 90 52 10, forgesleseaux-tourisme.fr, Mon-Sat 0930-1200, 1400-1800 (1700 Oct-Mar). Also Sun 0900-1300 from May to Sep.*

Lyons-la-Forêt

Hidden in the middle of the majestic beech woods of the Forêt de Lyons, romantic Lyons-la-Forêt is the main town in the Pays de Lyons – though in reality it is just a simple woodland village with a population of under 1000. It has had many historic royal and ducal connections, not least that Henry I of England died here following a meal of lampreys – a lamprey is a creature like a blood-sucking eel – at nearby Mortemer Abbey. Lyons makes an ideal base for exploring the region. With its old flower-decked half-timbered houses, especially the magnificent ensemble around the long, narrow wooden *halles* (covered market) in the main square, it is wonderfully picturesque all year round. Understandably, it attracts a lot of visitors. Perhaps the best time to visit is in autumn, when leaves have turned to bright colours and the busloads of summer daytrippers have departed. The village is at its quietest on Tuesdays and Wednesdays, when many of the shops are closed. There's a **tourist information office** ① *20 rue de l'Hôtel de Ville, T02-32 49 31 65, paysdelyons.com, Easter-mid Oct Tue-Sat 0930-1215 and 1400-1730, Sun 1000-1200 and 1400-1630; mid Oct-Easter Tue-Sat 1000-1200 and 1400-1700.*

Neufchâtel-en-Bray → *For listings, see pages 67-68.*

The capital of the Pays de Bray, though not its largest town (Gournay is larger), Neufchâtel gives its name to the locally produced heart-shaped cheese, which gourmets consider one of the greatest cheeses in France. Neufchâtel is also a centre for other Bray cheeses. There's a **tourist information office** ① *6 place Notre Dame, T02-35 93 22 96, neufchatel.fr, Tue-Fri 0930-1230 and 1400-1830, Sun in high season 1030-1230.*

Almost destroyed in the war, and rapidly rebuilt, it's not an especially attractive place. Yet it has a pleasant atmosphere, with good markets on Tuesday and Saturday mornings. The town's Eglise Notre-Dame on place Notre-Dame is an interesting old church and, in a 16th-century manor, the **Musée Mathon-Durand** ① *Grand'Rue St-Pierre, T02 35 93 06 55, Apr-mid Jun and mid-Sep-Oct Sun only 1500-1800, mid-Jun to mid-Sep Tue-Sun 1500-1800, closed Nov-Mar, €3, €1.50 child and concessions*, is a museum of regional arts taking a thorough look at ironwork, pottery and cider-making.

Neufchâtel makes a convenient starting point for trips into the Forêt d'Eawy (the name is pronounced Ee-aa-vee). This extensive mature beech forest lies west of the town, and is crossed by impressive walks and drives. North of Neufchâtel, the small Basse Forêt d'Eu and larger Haute Forêt d'Eu are similar mature beech woods reaching towards the Picardy border.

Just outside Neufchâtel in the direction of Dieppe, the 15th-century **Château de Mesnières-en-Bray** ① *T02 35 93 10 04, chateau-mesnieres-76.com. Easter to All Saints (1 Nov) weekends and national holidays; Jul-Aug open Wed-Mon. Open for 45-min guided tours only 1430-1830, €4 (park only, €2)*, was damaged by fire in 2004, and is still being repaired. With its white round towers under black slate roofs, and its fine Cour d'Honneur, it looks like a Loire château placed in the Norman countryside, and is indeed based on the Château de Chaumont on the Loire. The château and its grounds are in use as a college of horticulture and forestry. Just 4 km further on, the church at Bures-en-Bray has a twisted octagonal wooded spire. Although the brick façade is a post-war replacement, most of the church is 13th century and it contains 14th- to 16th-century sculpture.

Lyons and Bray listings

For hotel and restaurant price codes and other relevant information, see pages 10-14.

😑 Where to stay

Forges-les-Eaux *p65*
€€€ Forges Hôtel, des Sources, T02 32 89 50 57, forgeshotel.com. Prices are for full board: bed, breakfast, and dinner including drinks. The focal point of a complex beside a green park on the edge of town, this modern hotel with dark, stylish, comfortable interiors has swimming pools, lounges and spa treatments. It adjoins a casino with a smart restaurant where meals are included in your stay.

Lyons-la-Forêt *p65*
€€€€-€€€ Licorne, place Benserade, T02 32 48 24 24, hotel-licorne.com. This handsome half-timbered former coaching inn has been part of the Lyons scene since 1610. With friendly, genuine and attentive staff, furnishings and decor that combine tradition with elegance, and varied but comfortable rooms in grey tones (with exposed wooden beams), it remains a top place to stay in Upper Normandy. Its restaurant La Licorne Royale (see below) is also outstanding.
€€€ Grand Cerf, place Isaac Benserade, T02 32 49 50 50, grandcerf.fr. A comfortable traditional inn that has been here for centuries, Le Grand Cerf reopened at the end of 2009 after being extensively refitted. It's a sister hotel of classier near neighbour **Licorne**, whose acclaimed young chef Christophe Poirier also oversees the management of the **Grand Cerf**'s restaurant.
€€€-€€ Lions de Beauclerc, rue de l'Hôtel de Ville, T02 32 49 18 90, lionsdebeauclerc.com. Furnished with antiques, but equipped with modern comforts (including free Wi-Fi) and with a home-from-home feel, this brick-built hotel is also an antiques shop – as well as a restaurant and *crêperie*. Note a €5 price hike for Sat night stays.

Chambres d'hôtes
€€ Château de Fleury-la-Forêt, Lyons-la-Forêt, T02 32 49 63 91, chateau-fleury-la-foret.com. This imposing privately owned 17th-century mansion in elegant grounds is open to visitors, but also has 3 grandly furnished bedrooms let as unusual and modestly priced *chambres d'hôtes*. Breakfast is served in the fine historic kitchen.

🍴 Restaurants

Forges-les-Eaux *p65*
€€-€ Auberge du Beau Lieu, route de Montadet, 2 km from Forges-les-Eaux, T02 35 90 50 36, le-beau-lieu.fr. Thu-Mon for lunch and dinner (and Mon lunch between Easter and 11 Nov), closed Jan and part Feb. Good, thoroughly French fare is the order of the day here, featuring such delicacies as *foie gras*, frogs' legs and a good choice of wines. Eat on the shady terrace in summer, or enjoy cosy fireside dining in the cooler months, at this rustic restaurant in pleasant Bray countryside just outside Forges.

Lyons-la-Forêt *p65*
€€€€ La Licorne Royale, place Isaac Benserade, T02 32 48 24 24, restaurant-lyons.fr. Lunch and dinner. In one of the village centre's half-timbered houses, tables are richly laid in white napery, in elegant rooms where in one, for example, framed *Brassaï* photos are spaced around the wall. Imaginative high-quality cooking, including such dishes as a *fricassee* made with a poularde of the Dame Noire breed with girolles mushrooms, have won prestigious national awards for the chef, Christophe Poirier.
€€-€ Les Lions de Beauclerc, rue de l'Hôtel de Ville, T02 32 49 18 90, lionsdebeauclerc.com. Fri-Tue for lunch

and dinner. A comfortable traditional-looking country dining room serving such dishes as soups, snails, salads and fish of the day, it also places the emphasis firmly on *crêpes* and *galettes*, which can be eaten as the main course.

○ Shopping

Lyons and Bray *p63*
Markets
Most towns and villages throughout the region have street markets at least once a week. The local produce market is still held in the historic wooden Halles in the centre of Lyons-la-Forêt every Thu, Sat and Sun morning. In the Bray country, Forges-les-Eaux holds its market on Thu and Sun mornings, while at Neufchâtel-en-Bray the market is on Sat morning.

Lyons-la-Forêt *p65*
Farm shops
La Boutique des 4 Fermières, 5 place Benserade, T02 32 49 19 73. Mon 1000-1200 and 1430-1830, Thu-Fri 0930-1230 and 1430-1830, Sat 0930-1230 and 1430-1900, Sun 1000-1200, 1500-1830. At this store 4 women farmers sell local gourmet products and farm produce.

Seine Valley above Rouen

Napoleon declared that Paris, Rouen and Le Havre were "but a single town, whose main street is the River Seine." True, the mighty river, winding and twisting, is navigable all the way from the English Channel into the French capital, but along the way the Seine passes through very different lands, whose ancient differences persist to this day. From Rouen to the eastern edge of Normandy is all part of the Vexin, a historic region divided into two when Normandy came into being with the River Epte as its frontier. On one side of the Epte lay the Vexin Français, with Pontoise as its capital. On the other side of the river was the Vexin Normand, bone of contention between the French and the Anglo-Normans. It's thoroughly peaceful now, and is an interesting, attractive region of woods and farms. Along the north bank of the Seine, chalky white escarpments mark the edge of the river plain. Les Andelys, on the north bank, is the region's main centre. On the other side of the river, Vernon was constructed as a border town by Rollo, founder of the Norman duchy. Cross the Seine again and continue upriver to reach Giverny, home of the great Impressionist, Claude Monet. The village of Giverny, on the eastern border of Normandy, is where Claude Monet, the 'father of Impressionism', made his home after he became successful.

Giverny → *For listings, see pages 72-73.*

La Fondation Claude Monet

ⓘ *84 rue Claude Monet, T02 32 51 28 21, fondation-monet.fr. 30 Mar-1 Nov daily 0930-1800. €9.50, €5 students and children aged 7-12, €4 disabled, under 7s free. Discounted combined tickets available for a variety of other museums – see website. To avoid the long queues to get in, book your ticket online in advance. It's less crowded first thing in the morning or early or late in the season. On an Apr morning, you can have the place to yourself.*

Claude Monet's house, now a national monument, is officially known as La Fondation Claude Monet. He moved here in 1883 and at once began work creating the exquisite gardens behind his new home. He acquired an additional piece of land, on the other side of a lane adjoining the garden, and this is where the famous lily pond can be found, subject of dozens of paintings in his latter years. The interior of the house, simply fitted out and decorated with the Japanese prints that so interested Monet, is impeccably preserved and is a fascinating example of a home in 1926 (the date of Monet's death). Abandoned after 1926, the house fell into disrepair and the gardens went to seed for 50 years. In 1977 the Académie des Beaux-Arts moved in and spent three years restoring Monet's house and garden to their original condition.

Musée des Impressionismes

ⓘ *99 rue Claude Monet, T02 32 51 94 65, museedesimpressionnismesgiverny.com. Apr-Oct 1000-1800, last admission 1730, check for temporary closures. €6.50, €4.50 students/teachers/unemployed, €4.50 child 12 and over, €3 child 7-12, under 7s free.*

The Museum of Impressionisms is a quiet place to enjoy modern painting and a shaded garden. The curious name, with its plural, reflects the intention to explore not just the original Impressionists, but the impact of the movement and the artistic developments that followed it.

Les Andelys → *For listings, see pages 72-73.*

Les Andelys is two separate villages – **Petit Andely** on the bank of the Seine facing an island in midstream, and **Grand Andely** 1 km inland – that have merged to form a single small town. Grand Andely is now mostly modern, while Petit Andely is picturesque and historic.

Château Gaillard

ⓘ *T02 32 54 41 93. Mid-Mar to mid-Nov Wed-Mon 1000-1300 and 1400-1800. €3 child 10 and over, under 10s free.*

Rising high on the edge of a white riverside cliff next to the Les Andelys, Château Gaillard gives a superb view of the river in both directions. This is the white fortress built (and designed) by Richard the Lionheart in a single year, 1196. The position of the castle, its dashing whiteness, together with the speed with which it was raised, earn it the name *gaillard* – which suggest a bold, stylish swagger. It is reached by a 30-minute steep climb on a footpath from Petit Andely, or by car from Grand Andely. While all that remains is ruins, an impression of how daunting and well-defended the site was quickly becomes clear. The castle's main section stands closest to the cliff edge, while a second section protects the landward approach, and is itself heavily fortified. During Richard's lifetime, it served its purpose in discouraging any French incursions into Normandy. When Château Gaillard passed to King John, the French moved into Les Andelys and began a lengthy siege. They eventually found a way into the castle… the outfall from the latrines. Having taken it, they were free to advance on Rouen. In later years, Les Andelys prospered and was the site of a river toll, a chain stretched across the Seine preventing passage to any vessel that had not paid.

Vernon → *For listings, see pages 72-73.*

On the Seine's left bank, just 4 km downstream from Giverny, Vernon is a pleasant town somewhat overlooked by visitors, originally built as a border defence by Rollo, Normandy's first duke. You can get an attractive view of it from the river bridge, which arrives in the old heart of town. Especially photogenic is the Vieux-Moulin, standing in midstream, relic of an older bridge. The newer part of town is laid out with pleasant avenues. There is a **tourist information office** ① *Maison du Temps Jadis, 36 rue Carnot, T02 32 51 39 60, cape-tourisme.fr, May-Sep Mon-Sat 0930-130 and 1330-1800, Sun 1000-1200, 1400-1600; Oct-Apr closes 30 mins earlier on weekdays and closed Sun; Nov-Mar Mon-Sat 0930-1230, 1400-1700*, with information on the wider area around the town, including Giverny.

La Tour des Archives
① *T02 32 51 39 60. Apr-Sep Tue-Sun 0915-1215 and 1415-1830, Sun 1015-1215; Oct-Mar Tue-Sat 0915-1215 and 1400-1730.*
La Tour is the remnant of a castle, built after the French had taken Normandy. It's worth exploring, and the sentry walk gives another good view.

Musée Poulain
① *Rue Dupont, T02 32 21 28 09. Apr-Oct Tue-Sat 1030-1800; Nov-Mar Tue-Fri 14-1730, Sat-Sun 14301730. €6.50, €4.50 child 12-18 and concessions, €3 child 7-12.*
Vernon's museum covers local prehistory and art – and surprisingly is the only museum in the Eure *département* with any Impressionist paintings, as well as some post-Impressionists. Its highlights are works by Monet and Bonnard, but there is also a small Vuillard, and well worth seeing are works by the daughter of Monet's second wife, Blanche Hoschedé-Monet (1865-1947). Vernon has an old church with modern stained glass, and preserves a few fine half-timbered houses, one of the best of them being the Maison du Temps Jadis, which is now the tourist office.

Château de Bizy
① *T02 32 51 00 82, chateaudebizy.com. Apr-Nov Tue-Sun 1000-1200 and 1400-1800, €7.80, €5 child.*
Just on the edge of Vernon, the Château de Bizy is a masterpiece of 18th-century neoclassical architecture, with Regency woodwork and rich Gobelins tapestries. The château's park, with its statuary, fountains and ponds, has lovely walks.

Seine Valley above Rouen listings

For hotel and restaurant price codes and other relevant information, see pages 10-14.

🛏 Where to stay

Giverny *p70*
Chambres d'hôtes
€€-€ Le Bon Maréchal, rue du Colombier, T02 32 51 39 70. In Monet's day, this was the small bar where he used to enjoy a little drink with friends. Nowadays it's a small and friendly guesthouse with a cottagey feel, and 3 delightful, simple and uncluttered homely bedrooms. Outside there's a garden and, just a short stroll away, Claude Monet's house.

Les Andelys *p70*
€€€ La Chaîne d'Or, 27 rue Grande, place St-Sauveur, T02 32 54 00 31, hotel-lachainedor.com. Closed certain days of the week mid Oct-mid Apr, 3 weeks in Jan and some national holidays. On the Les Andelys waterfront, this creaky old 18th-century tollhouse takes its name from the revenues raised from the river tolls which it gathered. It's now a hotel and restaurant of great charm, with greenery cloaking the façade, a riverfront garden and elegant, comfortable bedrooms. The ground floor dining room with beams and a warm, comfortable atmosphere, has river views and delicate, imaginative cuisine.

Vernon *p71*
€ Evreux, place d'Evreux, T02 32 21 16 12, hoteldevreux.fr. A 17th-century mansion that's loaded with historic atmosphere and evocative decor, the **Evreux** is well placed in the town centre. A traditional, unpretentious family-run small hotel it offers rooms, arranged around an inner courtyard, that are simple, clean and comfortable. Staff are helpful and friendly, and the hotel has its own restaurant, **Le Relais Normand**.

🍴 Restaurants

Giverny *p70*
€€-€ Baudy, 81 rue Claude Monet, T02 32 21 10 03, restaurantbaudy.com. 30 Mar-1 Nov, daily 1000-2330. This 'historical restaurant', as it is called, with its distinctive patterned pink brick façade, provides lunch and dinner in folksy old-fashioned dining rooms with bare boards, gingham cloths and paintings hanging on the pale walls. It's renowned as a former hotel where countless well-known artists have stayed. Outside, there's a charming rose garden. Set menus offer classic simple French fare and salads.

Les Andelys *p70*
€€€-€€ La Chaîne d'Or, 27 rue Grande, place St-Sauveur, T02 32 54 00 31, hotel-lachainedor.com. 15 Apr-15 Oct Thu-Tue for lunch and dinner; 15Oct-15 Apr Thu-Sat, and Mon for lunch and dinner, Sun lunch only. On the Les Andelys waterfront, see Where to stay, above. There's a fine old dining room with rich fabrics, wooden beams, river views and set menus of clever, tasty and unusual dishes such as roast *magret de canard* with peaches and nectarines and a peach sauce. Lunchtime menus Wed-Fri are especially good value.

Vernon *p71*
€€ Le Relais Normand, place d'Evreux, T02 32 21 16 12, hoteldevreux.fr. Mon-Sat for lunch and dinner. A big stone fireplace, with stags' heads displayed on either side, together with white napery, upholstered chairs and wooden beams give charm to this restaurant in the Hôtel d'Evreux, an evocative 17th-century town centre mansion that's now a modest but atmospheric hotel. Good, classic French and traditional Norman cooking is served, and in summer can be eaten in the courtyard.

€ Le Bistro des Fleurs, rue Carnot, T02 32 21 29 19, bistrodesfleurs-vernon.jimdo.com. Tue-Sat for lunch and dinner, closed about 1 week in Mar, 3-4 weeks in Jul or Aug. As the name says, it's a bistro-style restaurant, with a bar, posters on the walls, and classic French dishes of the day chalked on a blackboard. Good cooking at modest prices.

Seine Valley below Rouen

Twisting wildly in its wide flat valley, the River Seine continues its erratic journey from Rouen to its estuary at Le Havre. On both banks rise old abbeys and fortresses, evoking the time, almost a thousand years ago, when this waterway was Normandy's main thoroughfare. The gaunt ruins of Norman castles like the Château de Robert le Diable (near Rouen) and Lillebonne (near Le Havre) lend a fairy-tale look to the scene in places. Even the last remnants of the once-great Norman abbey of Jumièges are redolent of the majesty and importance of those powerful monasteries. Another great church stands by the river at Caudebec-en-Caux, beside the graceful Pont de Brotonne, built in 1977. Almost all the towns and sights are on the north bank, as it was easier to harbour boats here. Up to the post-war period, the Seine presented a huge obstacle to land travellers; until the Pont de Tancarville was built in 1959, there was no bridge across the river between Rouen and Le Havre. Much of the way, the river skirts the mature woodlands of the Forêt de Brotonne, now protected as a Parc Naturel Régional. Close to Le Havre, the river broadens to become a vast estuary, and the eye is filled with that space and light which the first Impressionists longed to capture on canvas.

Visiting the Seine Valley below Rouen

Tourist information

Information about all the lower Seine valley area is available from **Office de Tourisme Caux Vallée de Seine** ① *place du Général de Gaulle, Caudebec-en-Caux, T02-32 70 46 32, tourismecauxseine.com, Apr-Sep 1000-1830 (opens 1100 on Sun); Oct-Mar Mon-Sat 1000-1230 and 1330-1700.* There are other branches at Lillebonne and Bolbec.

Caudebec-en-Caux → *For listings, see page 77.*

On the Seine's right bank, at the foot of the Pont de Brotonne, the small town of Caudebec was once a thriving river port. For centuries, one of the attractions of Caudebec and the 4 km of riverbank between here and neighbouring Villequier – at the Spring and Autumn equinoxes – was the *mascaret*, or tidal bore, that used to sweep up the Seine from Le Havre, getting higher and higher as the river narrowed. Often catastrophic (Victor Hugo's daughter and son-in-law were among the many who were drowned when they came to observe it), it was eventually brought under control in 1965 and no longer reaches great heights.

Caudebec was renowned too for its wealth of medieval half-timbered houses. When the town centre was set on fire by retreating Germans, almost all were destroyed, although a notable survivor of the flames is the lovely 13th-century Maison des Templiers (rue Basin) with its arcaded front. This history is told in the **Musée de la Marine de Seine** ① *av Winston Churchill, T02 35 95 90 13 (phone to check if the museum has reopened after scheduled reconstruction work).* Today the town is best known for its 15th- and 16th-century Flamboyant Gothic masterpiece, Eglise Notre-Dame. A few paces from the church is the place du Marché, where a market has been held every Saturday morning since 1390.

Eglise Notre-Dame

① *Rue Jean Prévost. Usually daily 0800-1800.*
"The most beautiful chapel in my kingdom," as Henri IV described it, has glorious intricately carved stonework inside and out, especially on the west façade. There is an early 16th-century organ, and superb 16th-century stained glass, including a fine rose window on the west front.

Abbaye de St-Wandrille

① *T02 35 96 23 11, st-wandrille.com. Daily 0515-1300 and 1400-2115, free.*
Standing in the countryside 2 km from Caudebec are the vestiges of the Abbaye de St-Wandrille, originally founded in the seventh century. Almost nothing survives of the Norman and medieval abbey buildings that stood here, except the 14th-century cloisters. However, the Benedictine order returned to the site in the 1930s; the monks' church is a former 13th-century tithe barn brought here from La Neuville-du-Bosc, in the Eure.

Château de Robert le Diable → *For listings, see page 77.*

On a hilltop behind the villages of La Bouille and Moulineaux, on the Seine's south bank, right beside Autoroute A13, rises the ruined castle of 'Robert the Devil'. Its towers and arches command an immense view over the river and all the Rouen area. There is no entry to the buildings, but the view rewards a climb. There is no historical record of anyone being known by the name Robert the Devil. Many suggestions have been made; the French

Ministry of Culture has noted that it may refer to Robert Courteheuse, Duke of Normandy from 1087 to 1096. The existing castle was originally a 13th-century reconstruction, altered again in the 14th century, and largely destroyed in the 15th. It was closed to the public in 2003, damaged by fire in 2007, but is currently being restored. Below the castle, the village of La Bouille is a pretty spot.

Jumièges → For listings, see page 77.

Abbaye de Jumièges
ⓘ *Rue Guillaume-le-Conquérant, T02 35 37 24 02, abbayedejumieges.fr. 15 Apr-15 Sep 0930-1830; 16 Sep-14 Apr 0930-1300, 1430-1730. Last entry 30 mins before closing. €5. Concessions €3.50. No animals.*

As soon as one steps among the extensive, majestic ruins of this legendary 10th- and 11th-century abbey, it's clear that they give only a hint of how impressive these monumental buildings of white stone must once have been. The abbey's churches were considered among the supreme examples of Norman architecture at its best. Just enough remains to set the imagination working, rebuilding walls and ceiling vaults, and visualizing roofs and doorways and windows that today are missing.

The ruins are of the abbey churches, the older St-Pierre and the principal church Notre-Dame. Many other structures, such as the cloisters, have completely vanished. However, a good deal remains of the west front of Notre-Dame and its two towers, and part of the older St-Pierre, where painted decoration can still be seen. The two churches are connected by a vaulted passage.

The original seventh-century abbey on the site was attacked so often by the Viking raiders, and so comprehensively stripped of its treasures, that it effectively ceased to exist until Rollo promised to repair the damage his people had done in exchange for having a duchy to call their own. The Normans created their own solid but elegant Romanesque style, and Jumièges was rebuilt in the 10th century. It suffered during the Hundred Years War, but it was the French – not the Vikings – who dealt the fatal blow to the abbey and its buildings, during the Revolution in 1789. The whole site was sold at auction in 1793 to a building supplies merchant. The destruction was undertaken systematically, using gunpowder to bring down, for example, the famed lantern tower. In 1852, the site was again purchased by private buyers, the wealthy Lepel-Cointet family, who tried to prevent further damage and preserve what remained, even restoring part of the site. They are credited with preventing the total destruction of the abbey, which they sold to the state in 1946.

Forêt de Brotonne (Brotonne Forest)
ⓘ *The forest is freely accessible at all times. Information from Maison du Parc, Notre-Dame-de-Bliquetuit (on south bank, 4 km from Pont de Brotonne), T02 35 37 23 16, pnr-seine-normande. com. The Maison du Parc is open Oct-Mar Mon-Fri 0900-1230, 1330-1800; Apr-Jun and Sep, Mon-Fri 0900-1800, Sat-Sun 1300-1800; Jul-Aug Mon-Fri 0900-1830, Sat-Sun 1000-1830.*

Much of the Lower Seine valley comes within the borders of the Parc Naturel Régional des Boucles de la Seine Normande (formerly the Parc Naturel Régional de Brotonne), which protects the diverse terrains on the riverbanks. The finest feature of the park is the huge Brotonne Forest, which once belonged to the monks at Jumièges Abbey. Most of the forest is a magnificent ancient woodland of beech, oak and pine. Paths and tracks, and roads too, allow for idyllic excursions among the shady trees. The village of La Haye-de-Routot on the southern edge of the forest, is a delightful haven of old woodland traditions and crafts.

Seine Valley below Rouen listings

For hotel and restaurant price codes and other relevant information, see pages 10-14.

⊖ Where to stay

Jumièges *p76*
€€€ Le Clos des Fontaines,
rue des Fontaines, T02 35 33 96 96,
leclosdesfontaines.com. Closed for 2
weeks over Christmas and New Year. Very
comfortable and well equipped, with many
attractive and romantic touches – rich
fabrics, 4-poster beds, wooden beams,
exposed brick – every room in this hotel
has its own distinctive character and colour
scheme. The smaller rooms have a pleasing
neat style, while the pricier junior suites are
positively sumptuous. Close to the abbey.

❼ Restaurants

Jumièges *p76*
€€ Auberge des Ruines, place de la Mairie,
T02 35 37 24 05, auberge-des-ruines.fr.
Lunch and dinner daily except Sun eve,
and Wed, closed 2 weeks end Aug, 2 weeks
Christmas/New Year, 1 week in Feb. An
utterly charming half-timbered restaurant

and outdoor terrace just opposite the
abbey, the emphasis is on simple but
high-quality gastronomic dining. Try,
for example, bass with mushroom oil
and garlic-flavoured crème chantilly.
€€-€ Auberge du Bac, rue Alphonse
Callais, T02 35 37 24 16. Wed-Sun 1200-1330
and 1900-2100. Half timbered, with hanging
flower baskets, and inside, a cosy rustic
ambience with old-fashioned chairs, tiled
floor, red and white cloths and copper
pans hanging on the walls, this attractive
riverside restaurant offers several set
menus of rich Normandy and French
cooking. There's plenty of fresh fish and
shellfish, and even a between-courses
sorbet Normand on most menus.

✪ Festivals

Caudebec-en-Caux *p75*
Fête du Cidre du Pays de Caux, **end of Sep
(not every year)**. At apple harvest time, the
big, jolly cider festival takes over Caudebec
for a day. There's cider making and tasting,
as well as traditional craftsmen and women
making and selling their wares, processions,
puppet shows and local folk music.

South of the Seine

South of the Seine, the land is almost as flat and open as on the chalky uplands north of the river, with high plains, wide fields and extensive forests. Here, though, the country is more varied, more rustic and with more places great and small that deserve a visit. Almost all lies within the *département* of Eure. Despite industrial pockets, it's a region of appealing down-to-earth rural life, with good traditional cooking. The land is scattered with agricultural towns and villages of interest, ruined castles and monastic sites. Above all, there is plenty of water, with flowing streams and river valleys edged by woods. The wide River Risle flows into the Seine near the estuary, soon after passing through Pont Audemer, where little waterways thread through the town centre. Up the valley from here, the ruined abbey of Le Bec-Hellouin is set above the river, with good views. Another enjoyable river journey is along the little Iton, a tributary of the River Eure, following it as far as Evreux, the local capital much scarred by war. From here yet another river, the Rouloir, skirts the forests of Evreux and Conches to reach the medieval pilgrimage town of Conches-en-Ouche.

Le Bec-Hellouin → *For listings, see pages 81-82.*

The little village of Le Bec-Hellouin (lebechellouin.fr), outside the abbey walls, rewards a stroll. Its half-timbered buildings are arranged in handsome terraces, and woods and fields climb the slopes to either side.

Abbaye Notre Dame du Bec-Hellouin (Le Bec-Hellouin Abbey)

ⓘ *T02 32 43 72 60, abbayedubec.com. Daily Jun-Sep, 1-hr tours at 1030, 1500, 1600 and 1700 (Sun 1200, 1500 and 1600), Oct-May tours at 1030, 1500 and 1600 (Sun 1200, 1500, 1600), €5, €3.50 concessions, under 18s (or under 26s if resident in France) free.*

The early history of this once-vast and wealthy abbey illustrates the close links between Normandy and England. Three abbots of Le Bec-Hellouin also became Archbishops of Canterbury, Lafranc in 1070, Anselm in 1093 and Theobald in 1138. From Le Bec-Hellouin also came bishops of Rochester and abbots of Westminster, Ely, Colchester, Battle, Chester and Bury St Edmunds. Set above the Risle, the abbey once dominated the valley, but today just a few scant remnants stand on the site.

Originally founded about 2 km downriver in 1034, on a little tributary called the Bec, the religious community moved to this site in 1060. By then it was already famous, because Lafranc, a leading theologian from Italy, had come here in search of simplicity and seclusion. Here he began teaching, and so established the renown of Le Bec-Hellouin. Lafranc's presence attracted other scholars, most notably Anselm of Aosta.

The abbey flourished and retained through the centuries its early reputation for scholarship and piety. So it remained until the Revolution, when Le Bec-Hellouin was abruptly closed and the community broken up. Soon after, the church and much else was pulled down. The best part of what remains are a great wall of the cloister with a 14th-century Gothic doorway, and the massive square 15th-century Tour St-Nicolas, which has been restored. In 1948, the land was returned to the Benedictines, who have once more established a community here.

The surviving 17th-century refectory has become the new abbey church. You may walk freely in its grounds, but the abbey is open only for the guided tours.

Conches-en-Ouche → *For listings, see pages 81-82.*

Locally known simply as Conches, this peaceful and agreeable village stands on a long, narrow promontory ringed by the River Rouloir, in a lovely woodland setting. It is a popular centre of hunting, shooting and fishing. Several medieval houses survive along rue Ste-Foy, near the elaborate Gothic Eglise Ste-Foy housing the relics of Ste-Foy herself. The remains of this child saint were brought here, seemingly stolen from the magnificent Benedictine abbey church built especially for them at Conques in the Aveyron in southwest France, by the adventuring local lord, Roger de Tosny. Exiled from Normandy – it is not known what his crime was – he went on campaign against the Moors in Spain, where it seems he made a name for himself as particularly savage. He was eventually granted permission to return to Normandy, and stopped at Conques on the way, taking the opportunity to acquire part of the saint's venerated relics.

The village church in which Roger de Tosny kept the relics was rebuilt in the 15th century, with later additions in the 17th century. Inside is much good sculpture and woodcarving, but its greatest feature is excellent 15th- and 16th-century stained glass, considered some of the best in France. Behind the town hall, gardens lead to stony ruins of the sturdy 11th- and 12th-century keep (closed to the public) of the De Tosny family, encircled by a footpath and illuminated at night. There's a **tourist information office** ① *place Briand, T02 32 30 76 42, conches-en-ouche.fr.*

Evreux → *For listings, see pages 81-82.*

The capital of the Eure *département* has been much scarred by war, to the point of being devastated by fire half a dozen times in its history and almost completely demolished by German bombing in 1940 and Allied bombing in 1944. Yet Evreux resiliently rebuilds and carries on. Today once again it is a vibrant town. Its modern centre, around place Général de Gaulle, is bright and pleasant. The nearby Promenade des Berges de l'Iton (Banks of the Iton Promenade) is a delightful riverside walk. Anything from the town's long history that did survive the war has been carefully preserved, including the 44-m-high 15th-century Tour d'Horloge in the main square, and, most notably, the 12th- to 17th-century Cathédrale Notre-Dame. Frequent repairs, in different centuries, have left the cathedral with a combination of architectural styles which is striking and oddly pleasing. There is a fine 16th-century wooden screen, and stained glass, some of which dates to the 13th century. There's a **tourist information office** ① *1ter place Général de Gaulle, Evreux, T02 32 24 04 43, grandevreuxtourisme.fr, open Mon-Sat 0930-1830, Sun 1000-1230 (mid Jun-mid Sep closed Sun).*

Pont-Audemer → *For listings, see pages 81-82.*

Don't be deterred by the modern development and the traffic encircling this ancient river port town. Its old centre is well preserved, with narrow streets lined with half-timbered houses, many with wrought-iron balconies decorated with flowers; and little canals and waterways, as well as an arm of the River Risle, making their way towards the main river and the old port. Here and there in the old town you'll see former tanneries, as Pont-Audemer was once a centre for high-quality leather goods. Wander the streets on the left bank to the principal church, Eglise St-Ouen, which has Renaissance stained-glass windows, as well as some vivid modern stained glass by Max Ingrand. Close by, the Pont sur la Risle crosses the minor branch of the Risle which passes through the town centre, and gives views of the waterside houses. There is an **Office du Tourisme** ① *place de Gaulle, T02 32 41 08 21, ville-pont-audemer.fr/tourisme, Mon-Sat 0930-1230 and 1400-1730, Jun-Sep, also open Sun 1000-1200.*

South of the Seine listings

For hotel and restaurant price codes and other relevant information, see pages 10-14.

⊖ Where to stay

Pont-Audemer *p80*
€€€ Belle Isle sur Risle, 112 route de Rouen, Le Baquet, T02 32 56 96 22, bellille. com. Just outside town (in the Rouen direction), standing on an island in the River Risle in its own 2 ha of grounds with lawns, roses and mature trees, this 19th-century manor house now serves as a country-house-style hotel. The bedrooms, all different in size and shape, are decorated in classic style, well equipped and furnished with period furniture. Leisure facilities include sports amenities, indoor seawater bathing and an outdoor swimming pool. There's a good restaurant (closed at lunchtime on Mon, Tue and Wed), serving French gastronomic cuisine in a conservatory or in the indoor dining room hung with large paintings and antique mirrors.
€€ Auberge de l'Abbaye, place Guillaume-le-Conquérant, Le Bec-Hellouin, T02 32 44 86 02, hotelbechellouin.com. Closed mid Dec-mid Feb. An 18th-century inn in the centre of this quiet and beautiful village, the Auberge looks over the village green and is replete with old Normandy character and rustic charm, with flower boxes, wooden beams, bare brick and a warm welcome. Rooms are simple, clean, adequately equipped and decorated in pale colours, with a home-from-home feel. The hotel also benefits from a good restaurant.

⊘ Restaurants

Le Bec-Hellouin *p79*
€€ Auberge de l'Abbaye, place Guillaume-le-Conquérant, T02 32 44 86 02, hotelbechellouin.com. Wed-Mon for lunch and dinner (Thu-Mon Oct-Mar), closed mid Dec-mid Feb. It's no surprise that locals come

from all the surrounding towns and villages to eat at this rustic, charming 18th-century restaurant, with beams, low ceilings and bare brick, in the pretty village centre. Cooking is traditional and reaches a high standard. Among the highlights is its *tarte au pommes*.
€€-€ Restaurant de la Tour, 1 place Guillaume-le-Conquérant, T02 32 44 86 15. Fri-Wed for lunch and dinner, except Wed dinner, and Mon dinner in winter. In the pretty heart of the village, this is an inexpensive place to enjoy a friendly welcome and a choice of quick, simple dishes and classic French and Norman cooking, such as *cuisse de canard au cidre* (leg of duck braised in cider). In fine weather, eat outdoors on the terrace.

Conches-en-Ouche *p79*
€ Le Cygne, rue Guilbaud, T02 32 30 20 60, lecygne.fr. Lunch and dinner (call to check first). Old wooden beams, tiled floors and rustic decor in different dining rooms give atmosphere in this good classic local restaurant specializing in *foie gras* and a selection of traditional French and Normandy dishes, well prepared and presented.

Evreux *p80*
€€€-€€ La Gazette, rue St-Sauveur, T02 32 33 43 40, restaurant-lagazette.fr. Tue-Fri lunch and dinner, Sat for dinner only, closed most of Aug. Stylish and contemporary looking inside and out, with intriguing soft lighting, soft colours and soft music in a building with exposed timbers, this elegant place is pricey but serves wonderfully imaginative good French cooking, such as trout in a potato-bread crust with spinach and herb cream.

Pont-Audemer *p80*
€€€ Belle Isle sur Risle, 112 route de Rouen, Le Baquet, T02 32 56 96 22, bellille. com. This ivy-covered manor house on a river island just outside town is a haven in

which to enjoy refined and relatively light French gastronomic dishes with intriguing combinations of flavours; for example, upside down pear tart with hot *foie gras* and *cassis* vinegar. Vegetarians are catered for. Choose between the conservatory or the indoor dining room hung with large paintings and antique mirrors.

🍸 Bars and clubs

Evreux *p80*
L'Abordage,1 av Aristide Briand, T02 32 31 86 80, abordage.net. A short distance west of Evreux town centre, by the Cora commercial centre, this is the place to hear a good selection of live rock, pop and indie bands and performers from around the world. The name means 'collision', and this concert hall stages a wide range of local and international contemporary music playing in 2 different spaces, as well as devoting the last weekend in Jun to the festival Le Rock Dans Tous Ses États (lerock.org).

🛍 Shopping

Le Bec-Hellouin *p79*
Art and antiques
Le Bec-Hellouin Ceramics and Crafts, Ateliers du Bec, Abbaye Notre-Dame du Bec-Hellouin, T02 32 43 72 60. When not at prayer, the monks of Bec-Hellouin spend their hours in workshops producing delicate, high-quality hand-made ceramics, porcelain and faience with elegant, striking designs and decoration. In particular, they make dinner services and chinaware, lamps,

vases and candleholders. Everything is for sale in their boutique at the abbey. Prices reflect the beauty and high quality, with items like dinner plates and salad bowls from about €25 each. Also on sale in the shop are unusual candles, CDs of liturgical music and books.

Evreux *p80*
Food and drink
Chocolatier Auzou, rue Chartraine, T02 32 33 28 05. Tue-Fri 09-1930, Sat 0800-1930, Sun 083013. This is a favourite spot for wonderful hand-made chocolates and mouth-watering soft macarons as well as an array of their own imaginative confections like *zouzous d'Auzou* and *pommes Calvados* (real Calvados inside!), and traditional local treats like *Caprice des Ursulines*. All should be sampled.

⊖ Transport

Pont-Audemer *p80*
Bus services are provided daily except Sun by Le Bus de Pont-Audemer; there are just 3 lines. There is no bus station, but the terminus is place Victor Hugo. ville-pont-audemer.fr/vivre-ici/bus.php.

ⓘ Directory

Pont-Audemer *p80*
Hospital Centre Hospitalier de la Risle (Pont-Audemer), 64 route de Lisieux, T02 32 41 64 64, ch-pont audemer.fr. **Pharmacy** Several in the town centre, including 2 in rue Thiers and 2 in rue de la République.

Contents

Footnotes

Language

Basics

hello	*bonjour*
good evening	*bonsoir*
goodbye	*au revoir/salut*
	(polite/informal)
please	*s'il vous plaît*
thank you	*merci*
I'm sorry, excuse me	*pardon, excusez-moi*
yes	*oui*
no	*non*
how are you?	*comment allez-vous?/*
	ça va?
	(polite/informal)
fine, thank you	*bien, merci*
one moment	*un instant*
how?	*comment?*
how much?	*c'est combien?*
when?	*quand?*
where is …?	*où est…?*
why?	*pourquoi?*
what?	*quoi?*
what's that?	*qu'est-ce que c'est?*
I don't understand	*je ne comprends pas*
I don't know	*je ne sais pas*
I don't speak French	*je ne parle pas français*
how do you say …	*comment on dit …*
(in French)?	*(en français)?*
do you speak English?	*est-ce que vous*
	parlez anglais?/
	Parlez-vous anglais?
help!	*au secours!*
wait!	*attendez!*
stop!	*arrêtez!*

Numbers

one	*un*
two	*deux*
three	*trois*
four	*quatre*
five	*cinq*
six	*six*
seven	*sept*
eight	*huit*
nine	*neuf*
10	*dix*
11	*onze*
12	*douze*
13	*treize*
14	*quatorze*
15	*quinze*
16	*seize*
17	*dix-sept*
18	*dix-huit*
19	*dix-neuf*
20	*vingt*
21	*vingt-et-un*
22	*vingt-deux*
30	*trente*
40	*quarante*
50	*cinquante*
60	*soixante*
70	*soixante-dix*
80	*quatre-vingts*
90	*quatre-vingt-dix*
100	*cent*
200	*deux cents*
1000	*mille*

Shopping

this one/that one	*celui-ci/celui-là*
less	*moins*
more	*plus*
expensive	*cher*
cheap	*pas cher/bon marché*
how much is it?	*c'est combien?/ combien ça coûte?*
can I have …?	*je voudrais…*
(literally 'I would like) …'	

Travelling

one ticket for…	*un billet pour…*
single	*un aller-simple*
return	*un aller-retour*
airport	*l'aéroport*
bus stop	*l'arrêt de bus*
train	*le train*
car	*la voiture*
taxi	*le taxi*
is it far?	*c'est loin?*

Hotels

a single/double room	*une chambre à une personne/ deux personnes*
a double bed	*un lit double/ un grand lit*
bathroom	*la salle de bain*
shower	*la douche*
is there a (good) view?	*est-ce qu'il y a une (belle) vue?*
can I see the room?	*est-ce que je peux voir la chambre?*
when is breakfast?	*le petit dejeuner est à quelle heure?*
can I have the key?	*est-ce que je peux avoir la clef?/ La clef, s'il vous plaît*

Time

morning	*le matin*
afternoon	*l'après-midi*
evening	*le soir*
night	*la nuit*
a day	*un jour*
a week	*une semaine*
a month	*un mois*
soon	*bientôt*
later	*plus tard*
what time is it?	*quelle heure est-il?*
today	*aujourd'hui*
tomorrow	*demain*
yesterday	*hier*

Days

Monday	*lundi*
Tuesday	*mardi*
Wednesday	*mercredi*
Thursday	*jeudi*
Friday	*vendredi*
Saturday	*samedi*
Sunday	*dimanche*

Months

January	*janvier*
February	*février*
March	*mars*
April	*avril*
May	*mai*
June	*juin*
July	*juillet*
August	*août*
September	*septembre*
October	*octobre*
November	*novembre*
December	*décembre*

Menu reader

General

petit déjeuner	breakfast
déjeuner	lunch
dîner	dinner or supper
hors d'œuvre	appetisers
entrées	starters
plat principal	main course
menu/formule	set menu
plat du jour	dish of the day
carte des vins	wine list

Drinks (*boissons*)

bière	German or Belgian-style beer
cidre bouchée	sparkling cider
cidre doux, cidre sec	dry cider, sweet cider
pommeau	strong apple aperitif
Calvados	apple brandy
apéritif	drink taken before dinner
digestif	*after-dinner drink, usually a liqueur or spirit*
eau gazeuse/pétillante	sparkling/slightly sparkling mineral water
eau plat/minérale	still/mineral water
bouteille	bottle
dégustation	tasting
vin rouge/blanc/rosé	red/white/rosé wine
pichet	jug, used to serve water, wine or cider
une pression	a glass of draught beer
une bière	a beer
un demi	small beer (33cl)
un cidre	cider
un panaché	beer/lemonade shandy
jus de fruit	fruit juice
orange pressée	freshly squeezed orange juice
sirop	fruit syrup or cordial served with water or soda
un coca	Coca-Cola
glaçons	ice cubes
un café	coffee (black espresso)
un (grand) crème	a (large) white coffee
une noisette	espresso with a dash of milk
deca	decaf
chocolat chaud	hot chocolate
lait	milk
un thé	tea, usually served black with a slice of lemon (au citron) – if you want milk ask for un peu de lait froid, a little cold milk
une tisane/infusion	herbal tea

Fruit (*fruits*) and vegetables (*légumes*)

ail	garlic
ananas	pineapple
artichaut	artichoke
asperge	asparagus
blettes	Swiss chard
cassis	blackcurrants
cèpes	porcini mushrooms
champignons de Paris	button mushrooms
châtaignes	chestnuts
chou	cabbage
citron	lemon
citrouille or potiron	pumpkin
cocos	small, white beans
courge	marrow or squash
épinards	spinach
fenouil	fennel
fèves	broad beans
figues	figs
fraises	strawberries
framboises	raspberries
haricots verts	green beans
lentilles vertes	green lentils
mesclun	a mixture of young salad leaves
poires	pears

pomme de terre	potato, primeurs are new potatoes, and frites are chips (chips being crisps)
pommes	apples, the Reinette d'Orléans and Reine des Reinettes are local varieties
prunes	plums
truffe	truffle

Sauces and cooking styles

dieppois	with mussels, white wine and cream
jus	meat juice with nothing added (may be thickened by reduction)
matelote Normande	creamy white sauce with cider and calvados
Normand(e)	cooked with cider or calvados, and cream added
à la Normande	casseroled with apples, calvados and cream
sauce	any kind of sauce or dressing
vallée d'Auge	meat flambéed in calvados and served in cream and cider sauce

Fish and seafood (*poissons et fruits de mer*)

aiglefin	haddock
anchoïade	anchovy-based spread
anchois	anchovies
anguille	eel
bar	bass
barbue	brill
bigorneaux	winkles
bulots	sea snails, whelks
cabillaud	cod
calamar	squid
coques	cockles

coquillage	shellfish
coquilles St Jacques	scallops
colin	hake
crevettes	prawns
dorade	sea bream
ecrevisses	crayfish
homard	lobster
huîtres	oysters
langoustines	Dublin Bay prawns
lotte	monkfish
loup de mer	sea bass
maquereau	mackerel
morue	salt-cod
moules	mussels
palourdes	a kind of clam
poissons de rivière	river fish
poulpe	octopus
poutine	very tiny, young sardines, most often cooked in an omelette or served raw
praires	clams
raie	skate
rascasse	scorpion fish
rouget	red mullet
St-Pierre	John Dory
sardines	sardines
saumon	salmon
soupe de poisson	a smooth rockfish-based soup
soupions	small squid
thon	tuna
truite	trout
turbotin	small turbot

Meat (*viande*) and poultry (*volaille*)

agneau (pré-salé)	lamb (from saltwater flood meadows)
andouillette	soft sausage made from pig's small intestines, usually grilled
à point	medium cooked meat (or tuna steak), usually still pink inside
bien cuit	well-cooked

blanquette de veau	veal stew in white sauce with cream, vegetables and mushrooms	*pintade*	guinea fowl
		porc	pork
		pot-au-feu	slow-cooked beef and vegetable stew
bleu	barely-cooked meat, almost raw	*poulet*	chicken
bœuf	beef	*rillettes*	coarse pork pâté
boucherie	butcher's shop or display	*rillons*	big chunks of pork cooked in pork fat
boudin	black pudding, blood sausage	*ris de veau*	sweetbreads
		sanglier	wild boar
canard	duck	*saucisse*	small sausage
charcuterie	encompasses sausages, hams and cured or salted meats	*saucisson*	salami, eaten cold
		saucisson sec	air-dried salami
		taureau	bull
		veau	veal
chevreuil	venison, roe deer		
confit	process to preserve meat, usually duck, goose or pork (eg confit de canard)	**Desserts (*desserts*)**	
		chantilly	whipped, sweetened cream
cuisse de grenouille	frog's leg	*compôte*	stewed fruit, often as a purée
dinde	turkey		
escalope	thin, boneless slice of meat	*crème anglaise*	egg custard
		crème brûlée	chilled custard cream dessert
faux-filet	beef sirloin	*crème caramel*	baked custard flavoured with caramel
foie-gras	fattened goose or duck liver		
		glace	ice cream
fumé(e)	smoked	*boules de glace*	scoops of ice cream
géline de Touraine or la Dame-Noire	grain-fed chicken prized by restaurateurs, awarded a Label Rouge	*le parfum*	flavour, when referring to ice cream or yoghurt
		pâtisserie	pastries, cakes and tarts – also the place where they are sold
gigot d'agneau	leg of lamb	*sabayon*	creamy dessert made with eggs, sugar and wine or cider
jambon	ham; look for jambon d'Amboise, an especially fine ham		
lapin	rabbit	*tarte au citron*	lemon tart
lardons	small pieces of ham	*tarte Normande*	apple tart
médaillon	small, round cut of meat or fish	*tarte Tatin*	upside-down apple tart
mouton	mutton	*teurgoule*	baked rice pudding sprinkled with cinnamon
pavé	thickly cut steak		

Other

assiette	plate (eg assiette de charcuterie)
beurre	butter
beurre blanc	buttery white wine sauce often served with fish
boulangerie	bakery selling bread and viennoiserie
brioche	a soft, sweet bread made with eggs and butter
casse-croûte	literally 'to break a crust' – a snack
une crêpe	pancake served with various fillings
croque-monsieur	grilled ham and cheese sandwich
croque-madame	as above but topped with a fried egg
crudités	raw vegetables served sliced or diced with a dressing, as a starter or sandwich filling
en croûte	food cooked in a pastry parcel
escargots	snails
forestière	generally sautéed with mushrooms
fromage	cheese
fromage de chèvre	goat's milk cheese
galette	savoury filled pancake made with buckwheat flour, served as a starter or main course
garniture	garnish, side dish
gâteau	cake
gaufre	waffle, usually served with chocolate sauce
Hollandaise	rich oil and egg yolk sauce flavoured with lemon juice
œuf	egg
pain	bread – choose from a rich variety of flavoured breads as well as the traditional baguette
pain au chocolat	similar to a croissant, but pillow-shaped and filled with chocolate
pâte	pastry or dough, not to be confused with pâtes, which is pasta or pâté, the meat terrine
riz	rice
rouille	saffron, garlic and paprika mayonnaise, served with soupe de poisson and bouillabaisse
salade verte	simple green salad with vinaigrette dressing
soupe/potage	soup
viennoiserie	baked items such as croissants and brioches

Index

Notes

Notes

Notes

Notes

Titles available in the Footprint *Focus* range

Latin America	UK RRP	US RRP
Bahia & Salvador	£7.99	$11.95
Brazilian Amazon	£7.99	$11.95
Brazilian Pantanal	£6.99	$9.95
Buenos Aires & Pampas	£7.99	$11.95
Cartagena & Caribbean Coast	£7.99	$11.95
Costa Rica	£8.99	$12.95
Cuzco, La Paz & Lake Titicaca	£8.99	$12.95
El Salvador	£5.99	$8.95
Guadalajara & Pacific Coast	£6.99	$9.95
Guatemala	£8.99	$12.95
Guyana, Guyane & Suriname	£5.99	$8.95
Havana	£6.99	$9.95
Honduras	£7.99	$11.95
Nicaragua	£7.99	$11.95
Northeast Argentina & Uruguay	£8.99	$12.95
Paraguay	£5.99	$8.95
Quito & Galápagos Islands	£7.99	$11.95
Recife & Northeast Brazil	£7.99	$11.95
Rio de Janeiro	£8.99	$12.95
São Paulo	£5.99	$8.95
Uruguay	£6.99	$9.95
Venezuela	£8.99	$12.95
Yucatán Peninsula	£6.99	$9.95

Asia	UK RRP	US RRP
Angkor Wat	£5.99	$8.95
Bali & Lombok	£8.99	$12.95
Chennai & Tamil Nadu	£8.99	$12.95
Chiang Mai & Northern Thailand	£7.99	$11.95
Goa	£6.99	$9.95
Gulf of Thailand	£8.99	$12.95
Hanoi & Northern Vietnam	£8.99	$12.95
Ho Chi Minh City & Mekong Delta	£7.99	$11.95
Java	£7.99	$11.95
Kerala	£7.99	$11.95
Kolkata & West Bengal	£5.99	$8.95
Mumbai & Gujarat	£8.99	$12.95

Africa & Middle East	UK RRP	US RRP
Beirut	£6.99	$9.95
Cairo & Nile Delta	£8.99	$12.95
Damascus	£5.99	$8.95
Durban & KwaZulu Natal	£8.99	$12.95
Fès & Northern Morocco	£8.99	$12.95
Jerusalem	£8.99	$12.95
Johannesburg & Kruger National Park	£7.99	$11.95
Kenya's Beaches	£8.99	$12.95
Kilimanjaro & Northern Tanzania	£8.99	$12.95
Luxor to Aswan	£8.99	$12.95
Nairobi & Rift Valley	£7.99	$11.95
Red Sea & Sinai	£7.99	$11.95
Zanzibar & Pemba	£7.99	$11.95

Europe	UK RRP	US RRP
Bilbao & Basque Region	£6.99	$9.95
Brittany West Coast	£7.99	$11.95
Cádiz & Costa de la Luz	£6.99	$9.95
Granada & Sierra Nevada	£6.99	$9.95
Languedoc: Carcassonne to Montpellier	£7.99	$11.95
Málaga	£5.99	$8.95
Marseille & Western Provence	£7.99	$11.95
Orkney & Shetland Islands	£5.99	$8.95
Santander & Picos de Europa	£7.99	$11.95
Sardinia: Alghero & the North	£7.99	$11.95
Sardinia: Cagliari & the South	£7.99	$11.95
Seville	£5.99	$8.95
Sicily: Palermo & the Northwest	£7.99	$11.95
Sicily: Catania & the Southeast	£7.99	$11.95
Siena & Southern Tuscany	£7.99	$11.95
Sorrento, Capri & Amalfi Coast	£6.99	$9.95
Skye & Outer Hebrides	£6.99	$9.95
Verona & Lake Garda	£7.99	$11.95

North America	UK RRP	US RRP
Vancouver & Rockies	£8.99	$12.95

Australasia	UK RRP	US RRP
Brisbane & Queensland	£8.99	$12.95
Perth	£7.99	$11.95

For the latest books, e-books and a wealth of travel information, visit us at:
www.footprinttravelguides.com.

Join us on facebook for the latest travel news, product releases, offers and amazing competitions:
www.facebook.com/footprintbooks.